A Mormon's Four-Step Journey to Holiness

How to Discover Purpose, Embrace Trials, and Align Your Life with God's Word

KENT EYNER NIELSEN

1st Editor: Wayne H. Purdin
2nd Editor: Katie Madsen Chambers
Formatters: Heidi Sutherlin
Cover Designer: Heidi Sutherlin

ISBN-10: 0-9976050-2-2
ISBN-13: 978-0-9976050-2-0

Matteo,

Thank you for the opportunity
visit today. It is mutually
to serve you. It is mutually
edifying to engage in the work
with a Brother in Christ!!

with love
& of good cheer

This book provides a refreshing approach to embracing the Gospel of Jesus Christ, and the LDS Faith. It promotes the acceptance of "Who we are" (A Child of God) as the foundational principle upon which our lives are designed and built. Without the acceptance of that one principle, we will maintain a journey of limiting beliefs, and limited success, in every area of our life, including financially. I especially appreciated the author's candid expository on his own journey that refined his personal view of who he is. Great Read!

**Tanya Faulk, Business and Financial Coach,
Falkon Business Management Services**

His courage in using very personal experiences to illustrate his journey toward greater spirituality is commendable ... [may it] give hope to those who ... deal with similar issues. The ... inspiring quotes and scriptures [are] especially valuable.

Layne Jensen

As an active Latter Day Saint have you struggled to know "what" else you could do to feel more satisfied with your spirituality? When we ask how to get closer to the Lord, be more like him, we hear the same answers—study the scriptures, pray, go to church, serve. But what if the answer were to do what you are doing better, with greater understanding. [This] book will give you a lot to think about along those very lines.

Mary Ann Johnson

He holds nothing back in this Four-Step guide on the Journey to Holiness. The examples from his own life soundly punctuate the pearls of wisdom and nuggets of truth gathered from many sources included in its pages. By opening his own soul to the view of the reader, his experiences are embedded in the memory and one comes away changed by the pathos of understanding more deeply, the parallels and uniqueness of each person's journey. Following the simple pattern presented in these pages will lead to greater understanding, greater joy, and of course, greater holiness.

Tammy Jensen

Dedication

This book is dedicated to my Mom and Dad. Thank you for bringing me into this world and loving me. Both of you are champions for my success. I love you!

Acknowledgments

First, I give thanks to all the honorable and holy individuals who have gone before me and shared their wisdom in the form of a written record. I give a special thanks to the authors of the personal development and religious genres. I also give thanks to those who personally know me and have influenced my life, especially my wife.

I give thanks to Bob Proctor for writing his book, *You Were Born Rich*. His use of Mormon Canonized Scripture gave me strength to publish a personal development book that expounds upon the Scripture of my faith—The Church of Jesus Christ of Latter-day Saints.

Many thanks to the Self-Publishing School, which provided a blueprint for me to follow in the creation of this book. Thanks also to those friends that gave me feedback on the title. And to Katie Madsen Chambers' suggestions for making my manuscript more readable.

And above all, to my Maker, the giver of life, to His Son Jesus Christ, the Redeemer, and to the Gift of the Holy Ghost, the testifier. With them I exist, I am redeemed, and I share what I know with you.

TABLE OF CONTENTS

Thank you for purchasing
A Mormon's Four-Step Journey to Holiness.
You can learn more about Kent on his blog and
YouTube Channel.
Please visit:

www.KentEynerNielsen.com

PREFACE

Studying and living the laws of success can bring us wealth, health, and relationships. Isn't that enough? Isn't that all one should seek for?

Think about the rich man who approached the Savior, asking, "What lack I yet?" He had lived the laws of success all his days, yet felt that something was missing. If you can relate to this story, this book is for you.

Recently, I saw a presentation where a young man drew a portrait of himself. This high school student was the captain of multiple sport teams, came from a wealthy family, drove a new car, and had a beautiful girlfriend. Everyone admired him.

Yet, this young man drew himself with a gloomy face. In his hand, he was holding a mask of his face with a smile. In everyone else's eyes, he lived the perfect life. Others would have thought, *There's no reason for him to be sad or gloomy, for he has everything.* But deep within his soul, he knew something was missing.

Much like the adopted child who yearns to know his biological parents, each of us longs to know our Maker. If we are living a life, no matter how successful, without knowing our Maker, something's wrong.

1

Some may never know their biological parents, but you and I can know our Maker. And we don't have to wait until some future day beyond our death. We can and ought to know Him now—in this life!

alma 32:34

The purpose of this life is to prepare to meet God. If we're not preparing to meet Him, we have our ladder leaning on the wrong wall. We may have all the glory of this world, but if we don't know our Maker, we have nothing.

I came to know my Maker in 1993 and have put my ladder on His wall ever since. Over twenty years later, I stand all amazed at what's become of me, and marvel at what lies ahead. With my ladder on the proper wall, I have overcome some major obstacles. *Hymn 193*

Obstacles that I thought were stumbling blocks became steppingstones. And they were placed in my path to draw me closer to Him. *("The power to ask for Mountains to climb")*

Before I knew my Maker, I lacked much. Having scored a 17 out of 36 on the ACT, I thought my lot in life was to own a McDonald's restaurant one day. I had no hopes of attending college.

Since reconciliation with God, I've served Him in Mongolia for two years as a volunteer missionary. I've married the woman of my dreams. I've been involved in collegiate student government. I've graduated with honors from one of the most difficult universities to get into in the West—Brigham Young University. I've learned to thrive, even with two major nervous breakdowns. I'm helping to raise four amazing children. I'm now helping others to live a Life on Fire.

It is my hope that by studying and implementing the 4-step journey to holiness, you will:

* come to know your Maker;

- receive the fruits of the Spirit, even peace in this world;
- tap into His power to live a life beyond worldly riches; and
- become holy.

Lacking knowledge of your Maker leads to a life void of fulfillment. You may have worldly assets, but will they go with you beyond the grave? Life is about more than living and receiving success in the terms of the world—it's a time to prepare to meet God.

I invite you to dive into this book. The 4-step journey will help you discover a deeper purpose, overcome your greatest fears, and push through trials of your faith. Through this journey, you will align your life with the word of God that you may become one with Him while yet in the flesh.

INTRODUCING
KENT EYNER NIELSEN

Why Kent?

In the spring of 1993, I came to know my Maker. Before this event, I confessed and resolved the sins of my youth before a Judge in Israel with faith in Christ. (I confessed my sins to my ecclesiastical leader and accepted Christ's Redeeming Atonement over a length of time).

I then received a patriarchal blessing from a man holding the priesthood after the holy order of the Son of God (a blessing given once in your life, usually in your teen years, to direct your life according to God's will).

One week later, I received a written copy of this blessing. As I read the first sentence of the third paragraph, my spiritual eyes were opened. In an instant, I had answers to my deepest yearnings.

I knew I was a child of God, and the ramifications of being His offspring filled me with joy and rejoicing. This love permeated my soul and opened my eyes to the potential of the human race.

Before this enlightenment, I thought my lot in life was to own a McDonald's Restaurant. After receiving this vision, I knew there was something more. But I didn't know what my calling was.

When I read a former United States Secretary of Agriculture address, my life changed. This man, Ezra Taft Benson, a man whom I believe to be a living prophet of God, said,

> Yes, men and women who turn their lives over to God will discover that He can make a lot more out of their lives than they can. He will deepen their joys, expand their vision, quicken their minds, strengthen their muscles, lift their spirits, multiply their blessings, increase their opportunities, comfort their souls, raise up friends, and pour out peace. Whoever will lose his life in the service of God will find eternal life (1988, para. 20).

We need to cry unto the Lord more often.

Matthew 16:25

This quote pierced my soul! I read between the lines with my sixth sense. It was spirit speaking to spirit.

point of change "the turning point" →

A life consecrated to the Lord would be more fruitful than anything I could imagine. To the invitation from the spirit of the Lord, which was to test the words of this man, I cried out, in Yoda like language, "Let Him I will!" This was an unalterable decision. I set out to prove the words of this prophet by living a life dedicated to the will of the Lord. *I went straight to action*

It's been over twenty years since that decision, and I marvel at what I've overcome and become. On my own, I would not be here today. But with the knowledge of my Maker, power from on High has helped me to overcome the trials that have beset me.

Faith Tried

In the spring of 2000, I faced my greatest fear. I was on top of the world. I had a nice car. I was going to a great university. I was to marry a beautiful woman. As a son of God, I felt invincible. But like Job, the adversary had power in my life based on my fear.

Job faced his fear. We read, "For the thing which I greatly feared is come upon me, and that which I was afraid of is come unto me" (Job 3:25).

The adversary tried the faith of Job. He thought he saw a space in his armor to place a wedge. But God knew better and said Job was a perfect man. Still, the adversary attempted to sway Job to the dark side.

For some reason, the adversary still fights against the Father, as if he doesn't know God's word must come to pass.

So what effect did the adversary's trials have on the man Job? They brought Job to greater humility, greater power, and greater blessings.

My greatest fear was facing mental illness as many dear to me had faced. To avoid my fear, I became overzealous with my faith. I strove with due diligence to obey every law and to receive every rite I knew of. I studied, learned, and applied the doctrine of the gospel of Jesus Christ in my life.

Seeing fear in my life—a weak link in my armor—the adversary attempted to mislead me. In the spring of 2000, I was diagnosed with mental illness. This reality shook my world. In the depths of humility, I was brought closer to my Maker (see Chapter 6).

Mountains to Climb

Every 6 months, prophets and apostles speak to the world. In April 2012, an apostle of the Lord Jesus Christ, Henry B. Eyring, taught why he asked for mountains to climb. In October 1979, Eyring heard a prophet he admired say he was following the teaching found in the Old Testament (see Joshua 14:12). This man, Spencer W. Kimball, said,

There are great challenges ahead of us, giant opportunities to be met. I welcome that exciting prospect and feel to say to the Lord, humbly, 'Give me this mountain,' give me these challenges... Earnestly and fervently I urge that each of you make this same pledge and effort. (Kimbal 1979, 79)

Eyring accepted the challenge. "One night, I prayed for a test to prove my courage," said Eyring. "Within a day or two," his answer had come (2012, para. 2).

Almost a year after hearing Eyring's address, I plead for mountains to climb. Within a month, I was contemplating withdrawing from MBA school and considering suicide. In retrospect, I'm amazed that I dropped to this level of thinking.

For years, I had studied suicide. When I was about ten-years-old, my grandfather committed suicide. By my early twenties, more than one person near me had attempted suicide.

I knew that suicide was wrong, for it was like murder. Yet, I still contemplated it. It was as if I had forgotten about the mountains I had just prayed for!

With a support system, including my beloved wife, I didn't lay out a suicide plan. I knew this season would pass, but I was still perplexed.

The reason I contemplated suicide was due to my inadequacy to provide for my family. I had acquired another $40,000 in debt for MBA school. And now I was thinking of withdrawing from school.

As I continued to search for answers, a revelation came. In the revelation, I connected my new $40,000 debt to Esau's hunger (see Genesis 25:29-34). *The Man who sold his birthright for food*

This revelation shocked me. For $40,000, I was contemplating giving up my birthright when, like Esau, I had the potential to receive one hundred fold and more, and all this over my lack of vision.

I couldn't see how to provide for my family, nor how to pay my debts. But with this new insight, I cast out the notion of suicide and pressed forward with faith in Christ. If the lilies of the field receive their raiment, my family and I would have our needs and wants provided for.

Knowing I was not called to complete MBA school, I withdrew. Then I began the search for my calling.

Over the next year, I had five jobs, until I landed a job in the nonprofit sector. This was a godsend.

I figured that if I spent ten years working in this industry, my student loans would be no more. I passionately helped others give to those who were in need.

Promoted in less than a year, I felt I was in a sweet spot. I was working 32 hours a week. With the spare time outside of work, I continued to study and grow. Through this study, I came to know my calling.

The plan was to continue to work at this nonprofit organization, while working my calling on the side. Then I found failure. The new director called me to her office and let me go.

When I came home to tell my wife the news that I was no longer employed, I said, "I don't know if I should jump up and down for joy or cry." We chose the former and took it as a call to action to move forward with my calling in life.

The words of Andrew Carnegie ring true.

My experience has taught me that a man is never quite so near success as when that which he calls "failure" has overtaken him, for it is on occasions of this sort that he is forced to think. If he thinks accurately, and with persistence, he discovers that so-called failure usually is nothing more than a signal to re-arm himself with a new plan or purpose (Hill 2011, 19).

Recognizing God's hand in all things, I have taken up my calling, in part, to write this book.

It's invigorating to study and write. This form of spiritual exercise lights me on fire! After twenty years of living a life of consecration, it's my privilege to share with you what I've gleaned.

Thank you for sharing this experience with me. May you join me on a journey to mastery, a trip that involves climbing mountains.

I love hiking / Rock climbing so this should be a fun journey right?

Should

Introducing
The 4-Step Journey

Each section of this book lays out another part in the 4-step journey to holiness. Within each section, there are four chapters (one for each step).

The 4-Step Journey to Holiness

Here's the formula for the 4-step journey:

1. What?
2. Why?
3. How?
4. What to become? (Then Repeat)

In the following symbol, you will find the 4 steps depicted:

Let's start with the white triangle that would be a pyramid if it were a sphere. At the top of the triangle would be the question what. At the bottom right of the triangle would be the question why. And at the bottom left of the triangle would be the question how.

Next let us turn to the circle or sphere. Notice the three arrows pointing in clockwise motion. These arrows symbolize constant movement or action. This action is moved by questions. When there are questions, there are answers.

One of the most popular phrases in Scripture is "Ask and you shall receive, knock and it shall be opened, seek and you shall find" (Matt. 7-7). This is not by accident. When we ask questions of God, we invite inspiration to enter our hearts and minds (see D&C 6:11, 14-15).

There is a second meaning of the circle as well. If each of the corners of the triangle represented dots, the circle connects those dots. With the Spirit of God, these connections are made.

The great imitator, even the adversary, seeks to create a perfect circle, but he cannot. He lacks the Spirit of God. Without that Spirit, you cannot have a perfect circle.

The adversary will use the points of multiple triangles to teach a truth that looks like a circle. For example, after you superimpose triangle upon triangle upon triangle (say 100 of them) the outer points of the triangles would be in the shape of a circle. Without a line connecting the corners of the combined triangles or dots, it would not be a circle.

When you look at the symbol shared in this chapter, you will see some superimposed triangles. If the points of the triangle were dots, they are connected with three basic questions that look like arrows: "What?" "Why?" and "How?"

With the right questions, connecting the dots invites inspiration and revelation to make a perfect circle. The only way to connect the dots in a perfect circle is through the Spirit of God, which comes by inquiry.

Again, the three basic questions to teach the 4-step journey to holiness are "what," "why," and "how?" Answers to these three questions lead to the fourth question, "what to become?" The answer of what to become is a new "what," which is the beginning of the 3 basic questions again.

Liken this circular process to the thread on a bolt. First you have to align the bolt with a secured nut. The more you ask and receive answers, the deeper the bolt threads into the nut until the perfect day when the bolt is secured and welded in place.

Notice this journey or process is one that continues over and over unto perfection.

1. What? Quick to Observe—
An Inquisitive Mind.

Inquiry is the ignition switch to activate the circle of truth. The inquiry I'm referring to is not just asking but it is doing. As Stephen R. Covey puts it,

Share with your loved ones what you are learning. And most important, start applying what you are learning. Remember, to learn and not to do is really not to learn. To know and not to do is really not to know. (2004, 12)

When we do what we have learned, we gain knowledge. It becomes knowledge when you see the fruits of living what you have learned.

The only way to know something is to live it. As taught by our Savior, "If any man will do his will, he shall know of the doctrine, whether it be of God, or whether I speak of myself" (John 7:17).

The first step is having an inquisitive mind, which is a result of being quick to observe. Upon observing the fruits of others you admire, you could ask why or how they developed those fruits. With emulation of their answers, you would be on the fast track to developing similar fruits.

Inquiry is the key to understanding things as they really are, have been, and will be:

> *And if thou wilt inquire, thou shalt know mysteries which are great and marvelous.... Verily, verily, I say unto thee, blessed art thou for what thou hast done; for thou hast inquired of me, and behold, as often as thou hast inquired thou hast received instruction of my Spirit. If it had not been so, thou wouldst not have come to the place where thou art at this time. Behold, thou knowest that thou hast inquired of me and I did enlighten thy mind; and now I tell thee these things that thou mayest know that thou hast been enlightened by the Spirit of truth. (D&C 6:11, 14-15)*

Asking is the key to activating the Spirit to teach you the correct answers. It is "by the power of the Holy Ghost [that] ye may know the truth of all things" (Moroni 10:5).

Again, looking at the symbol, the top outer point of the triangle is "what?" Answering what is observed leads to the following question of "why?" Which leads to the next question "how?"

Connecting these questions is done by inspiration from on

High. It is God's Holy Spirit communicating to our spirit.

When we're quick to live what we observe, we'll be inspired with the right questions. The first time I felt inspired with the right questions was when I was 19 years old. I was in the Missionary Training Center in Provo, Utah. My teachers taught me that the Spirit would literally fill my mind with questions to ask.

One evening I was waiting outside of a classroom reading my scriptures. Some of my fellow missionaries were teaching an ESL (English as Second Language) class. When the class was over, several students came out and surrounded me. I was sitting at a desk. They started asking me questions. This was my first experience talking to anyone about the gospel.

One of the students stood out and I felt inspired to ask him certain questions. Questions I had never asked anyone before. For example, I asked him, "Do you have access to the Book of Mormon?" And "Have you ever read the Book of Mormon?"

His response revealed that he had access to the Book of Mormon and had read some of it. I was then prompted to ask him if he had prayed about it.

Remember, these young adults were ESL students. I didn't know this young man's native tongue. So our conversation was in broken English.

As he answered my inquiries, I learned that he had attempted to pray about the Book of Mormon. Furthermore, he confessed that he didn't know how to pray. I then took courage to ask if he would like to learn how to pray.

"Yes, I learn pray," was his response. I could barely contain myself. I jumped up and got my companion and we went into a room to teach him how to pray.

This experience amazed me! There is more to asking than just saying, "What?" It is observing something good, asking inspired, sincere questions, and acting upon the answers. Ask that you may receive.

However, in asking, you need to ask good questions rather than poor questions. Tony Robbins teaches that if you ask a poor question, you're going to get a poor answer.

Poor question example: Let's say I played basketball yesterday morning. If I struggled making my shots, I could have asked the former basketball coach I was playing with, "What's wrong with me?" To which he could have pointed out all my faults, not to mention my own negative thoughts. In both cases, I would have received what I asked for, which could have sent me down a negative spiral.

Good question example: "Hey, Coach, what can I do to improve my shot?" For this question, I would have received advice on how to improve my accuracy in shooting. He could have said something like, "You need more arc in your shot" or "Work on bank shots to increase confidence."

The poor question would have supported my negative thinking; whereas, the latter question would have given me courage and confidence with the response.

Being quick to observe is to notice talents that others have. Recognizing talents allows us to complement and learn from others. One with an inquisitive mind could take courage and ask that person how they lay hold of their talent(s). Upon receiving the answer, we have the opportunity to follow the advice. Acting on this advice opens the door for us to enjoy the same fruits.

Observing good is an answer to the first question, "what?" The next question to ask is "why is it good?" or "why is it what it is?"

2. Why? An Innate Desire to Know Truth!

Have you ever noticed an adopted child usually wants to know who their biological parents are, even if they've heard bad stories about them? They just want to know. They want to know whom they look like. They want to know what they're doing, how they got where they are, etc.

There is an innate desire to know where we come from. Like the adopted child, I believe each of us desires to know our Maker. As His offspring, we innately desire to learn of Him and desire to be like Him.

We are beings of light and truth and, as such, we thrive on learning more light and truth or laying hold of every good thing. Why we thirst for more is described well in the following scripture: "For intelligence cleaveth unto intelligence; wisdom receiveth wisdom; truth embraceth truth; virtue loveth virtue; light cleaveth unto light" (Doctrine and Covenant 88:40).

"Intelligence" in its purest form is not doing well on a man-made IQ test; it "is light and truth," even "the Glory of God" (D&C 93:36). As His children, we are intelligences, too. Thus, we are attracted to cleave unto further light and truth as it comes to us. This is the great "why."

3. How? Revelation is Spirit Talking with Spirit.

To receive answers to our deepest yearnings, we must ask, knock, and seek with inquiry and action. Do not confuse the things of the Spirit with the lusts of humans. As beings of spirit, we control our physical bodies with our spirit. The physical is but a vehicle.

Stephen Covey quotes Teilhard de Chardin as saying, "We are not human beings having a spiritual experience. We are spiritual beings having a human experience" (1989, 319).

As beings of spirit, we can be a receptacle of the purest form of communication, even revelation. "For what man knoweth the things of a man, save the spirit of man which is in him? Even so the things of God knoweth no man, but the Spirit of God" (1 Corinthians 2:11).

When we receive revelation, we have an opportunity to use agency. We can accept and test out this new truth or not. When we live by the new truth, we will receive fruits of the Spirit (see Galatians 5:22-23).

The fruits of the Spirit will cause our bosom to burn and fill us with joy, which allows our hearts to swell. Moreover, when we listen to the counsel to do good, we are filled with power to overcome.

When we reject the revelation and put it not into practice, we lose the power of that truth. Rejecting it shrinks our hearts and our ability to receive more revelation is stunted. (see Alma 12:10-11).

4. What to Become? (Then Repeat the Steps). Be Ye Holy.

When we accept and live by revelation, we learn the final step of what to become, even Holy. This "what to become" is another observation, which is the beginning of the 4-step journey again. When we continue to inquire after the good, we receive more and more revelation. It is written: "If thou shalt ask, thou shalt receive revelation upon revelation, knowledge upon knowledge, that thou mayest know the mysteries and peaceable things—that which bringeth joy, that which bringeth life eternal (D&C 42:61).

By receiving more and more revelation, and living it, we become Holy! As offspring to the Most High, we are entitled and commanded to be holy. This is not a new topic. It comes from ancient text. Here is an example of what is written,

> *For I am the Lord your God: ye shall therefore sanctify yourselves, and ye shall be holy; for I am holy ... For I am the Lord that bringeth you up out of the land of Egypt, to be your God: ye shall therefore be holy, for I am holy. (Leviticus 11:44-45)*

The notion of what to become is the beginning of a new 4-step journey. Next, ask, "Why is this so?" Then ask, "How is it possible?" You'll be led to the answer to the question, "what to become?" Follow the response with action and further inquiry!

In this book, we will figuratively peal back layers of an onion on this 4 Step Journey to Holiness. Going through the 4-part journey four times, we will discover what to become in each step 4, and this answer will then lead us to a new what.

Section 1

Seek Wisdom

Seek not for riches but for wisdom; and, behold, the mysteries of God shall be unfolded unto you, and then shall you be made rich. Behold, he that hath eternal life is rich (D&C 11:7).

As a boy, I didn't learn to read until sixth grade. Reading was a chore rather than a joy. I did just enough to pass high school with a 3.0 GPA. I read CliffsNotes and watched movies on the assigned readings.

By the age of nineteen, I had read about three books cover to cover, not including a few choose-your-own-adventure books. I was an audio learner and a slow reader. Watching an hour and a half movie made more sense than spending hours slugging away at a book.

In my eighteenth year, I tapped into the power of books filled with wisdom. The first book I read was the *Book of Mormon*. It took me weeks to start reading and over a year to complete.

My ecclesiastical leader challenged me to read the *Book of*

Mormon. I accepted and sat down to read it. I couldn't complete the first page. It didn't make sense to me; I didn't understand it.

A week passed and I reported to him. He asked if I had said a prayer before I read it. I told him I hadn't and committed to do so.

That week, I commenced my reading with a prayer. I still got the same results. The following week, I reported, and he asked, "What do you think the scriptures are?" I replied, "They're a list of commandments of things to do and not to do." He got a good chuckle out of my explanation. He then taught me that they were a collection of journal entries, entries from holy men, even prophets, who shared the stories of their lives.

He then challenged me to start the *Book of Mormon* again. But this time, with more than a prayer. He said, "Imagine you're with these men as their story unfolds, meaning that when Nephi builds a ship, imagine yourself next to him. You're handing him his tools as he builds it." After his explanation, I thought, "I could do that ... for it would be just like helping my dad build a fence."

Reading from this vantage point opened my eyes! I discovered holy men who knew their Maker. And they were sharing with me, a poor, uneducated boy, the greatest mysteries in the world. Within a year and a half, I was serving the Lord in Mongolia as a volunteer missionary, creating my own journal.

While in Mongolia, the genre of personal development books came to my attention. I read books like:

- Stephen Covey's How to Succeed with People;
- Stephen Covey's Spiritual Roots of Human Relations; and
- Dale Carnegie's How to Win Friends and Influence People.

I couldn't believe it. These modern wise men were sharing their wisdom with me! Hooked for life, I then loved reading. Books opened the door to wisdom. They taught me how to find my calling.

My Calling

When asked as a boy, "What would you like to do?" I responded, "I don't know; what about you?" Most boys would say something like, "a businessman," "a lawyer," "a doctor," or "a professor."

When I followed up with, "What does your dad do?" The majority would say their dad did the same thing they wanted to do.

My dad was a truck driver who was gone five to six days a week. I didn't want to be a truck driver. Not knowing what my options were, my default answer was, "I don't know."

When I was sixteen, a store manager of a McDonald's restaurant took me under his wing and sold me on his dream. He wanted to own his own McDonald's franchise one day. He then shared the financial numbers with me. (All I remember was it was in the millions for just one restaurant and the owner owned several!) Elated with the notion of being a millionaire, I bought into his dream. I wanted to own a McDonald's restaurant.

In my eighteenth year, I learned I could square my life with the Lord. When I did square my life with Him, my eyes were opened to a part of His glory. In a sacred moment, I saw the potential of the human race and the love of God.

I have now spent the last twenty years living a consecrated life, discovering my calling and using my unique gifts. These gifts were not given to help run a McDonald's chain. They were not given to obtain an MBA degree. They were given to help others draw nearer to God.

In the following four chapters, we'll dive into the first part of the 4-step journey to holiness—seek wisdom.

CHAPTER 1

I will praise personal development in this chapter. But, at the same time, I will expose the limitations of our finite desires. Personal development in conjunction with "thinking big" is essential. But as mortals, however big our thinking is, it's not big enough. We must think divine thoughts to live a Life on Fire!

Step 1: What?

Personal Development = Reaching for More

As an American studies major in college, I did a research paper on the American dream. The American dream is the typical rags to riches story, so I thought. To my surprise, this wasn't what others thought.

In my research, those who I studied, rich or not, felt like they were living the American dream. Each of them had laid hold of their desires. For some, that was an education; for others, it was employment, or it was home ownership and a family. This was their American dream.

The beauty of the personal development genre is that it

teaches you how to achieve what you want. Whether it be better relationships, better health, or more money, there's a book to teach you.

Personal development books often teach us the wisdom needed to fulfill our desires. The best books teach the significance of following universal laws and principles. They teach us to become more and to reach for more.

The Paradox of More

"The more I know, the more I realize I don't know anything," is a popular saying. The notion of learning more is good. But "ever learning, and never able to come to the knowledge of the truth" is not good (2 Timothy 3:7). "To come to the knowledge of the truth" is to come to know God.

We could follow the formula of book after book to get whatever we desire. But if doing so does not lead to a knowledge of the truth, we will feel a void.

Reality is the state in which God exists. If we're not coming to a knowledge of the Truth, we'll fall short of Reality. For Truth is God!

There are many good and honorable things to do, to give, and to receive in this life. Even so, if one doesn't strive to come to know his Maker, he will not receive a fullness of Joy. I'm not saying, "know of" his Maker, but "know" his Maker face to face.

Like an adopted child yearning to meet his or her biological parents, each of us has an innate desire to know God.

When we know our Maker, we too seek more and more. Those who say, "We have enough," from them "that which they have" will be "taken away" (2 Nephi 28:30).

Seeking gain for your personal kingdom will also lead to a void in life. However, seeking to glorify God's kingdom empowers you one hundred fold and more.

The folly of personal development is that it asks, "What do you want?" It will then proceed to tell you how to get it. What if you only wanted to own a McDonald's restaurant but you could have had eternal life by knowing God?

No matter how big our mansion is, if we don't know God, we'll feel a void. "For what is a man profited, if he shall gain the whole world, and lose his own soul?" (Matthew 16:26).

Not knowing God is to not know ourselves or our potential. "If men do not comprehend the character of God, they do not comprehend themselves" (Smith, p. 40).

Living on Fire = Feeding the Soul

We often think of feeding our physical body. As eternal beings, offspring of God, we need to feed our souls as much as we need to feed our bodies.

If we don't feed ourselves when we get hungry, we lose physical strength and stamina. Likewise, if we don't feed our souls spiritually, we starve and lose power to be wise. We do this by studying and implementing wisdom found in the best books.

Recently, I was watching a video from T. Harv Ecker. He points out the difference between successful people and unsuccessful people. His argument is that successful people have a filing cabinet in their heads full of wise decisions. These decisions come from personal experience or from books they've read.

The root of successful living is found in this filing cabinet. Feasting upon and living wisdom found in the best books will catapult your understanding. You can then make quantum leaps. Those who learn only from personal experience could be stuck in a rut, lacking access to wisdom.

When I do not fill my mind with the best books, including holy writ, depression sneaks in. I've found that to be a spiritual giant, you have to feast upon spiritual food. To fuel a Life on Fire, one must study and then apply what is learned.

When speaking of fire, two thoughts come to mind. The first is a biography on Ralph Waldo Emerson. The second is a quote from a former trainer.

In the concluding chapter of *The Mind on Fire*, Robert D. Richardson, Jr. shares two powerful Emerson quotes:

1. Stars ... are the most affecting symbols of what man should be. A spark of fire is infinitely deep, but a mass of fire reaching from earth upward into heaven, this is the sign of the robust, united, burning, radiant soul.
2. We must have not only hydrogen in balloons and steel springs under coaches, but we must have fire under the Andes at the core of the world.

I love this imagery. We ought to be stars, even radiant souls who at the core are lit with Fire.

The other idea came from my training as a ladder salesman. My trainer taught me, "If you light yourself on fire, people will come from miles and miles away, just to watch you burn!"

He also suggested that many will ask about your faith as you sell, because you're speaking truth. He even suggested that some will think you're a preacher, even though you're selling ladders. After a year and a half of selling, I found what he taught to be true. I sold many ladders and was often asked about my faith.

It is imperative to live a Life on Fire. Enthusiasm means "God within"; it is the key to living with passion. To have God within, we need to comprehend Him, and thus comprehend ourselves.

When I came to know God and my relation to Him, I discovered the seeds of greatness planted within my soul. Brigham Young put it this way,

> *The greatest lesson you can learn is to learn yourselves. ... You will then begin to learn more perfectly the things of God. No being can thoroughly learn himself, without understanding more or less of the things of God: neither can any being learn and understand the things of God, without learning himself: he must learn himself, or he never can learn God. (1860, 334-335).*

Let us continue to add fuel to our fire by study and action according to what we are gleaning from our studies. By feeding our souls consistently, we will maintain a spiritual high and live a Life on Fire.

In this chapter, we discussed the **what** in seeking wisdom: seek personal development in conjunction with the divine. While personal development aids our journey, we cannot rely solely upon our finite thinking. We need to tap into the divine by coming to know God. This will stretch our vision.

Personal development, without the divine, is like a marriage vow that's "until death do we part." It is finite.

Personal development, in conjunction with the divine, is like a marriage sealed with God's power for time and all eternity. It is infinite.

David J. Schwartz's book, *The Magic of Thinking Big*, sums

up the significance of thinking big. He suggests, "Big men do not laugh at big ideas" (Schwartz 1959, 121). As children of The Most High, it is imperative that we think beyond worldly riches. We're here to think divine thoughts.

In the next chapter, we'll discuss **why** divine thoughts are essential on our journey to holiness.

CHAPTER 2

In the preceding chapter, we discussed the need to tap into a divine source, lest we fall short of glory. Man, as great as he is, is nothing compared to the Glory of God.

Reading all the self-help books available will fall short of "gaz[ing] into heaven five minutes" (Smith 2007, 419). Study of the best books along with holy writ opens a conduit to receiving pure light and truth from on High.

This chapter will discuss the power of bringing all light and truth into one great whole. It's an invitation to see and live things as they really are, have been, and will be.

Step 2: Why?

Pure Light and Truth = Receiving Reality

Earlier, I wrote that "reality is the state in which God exists." Years ago, I overheard some guys discussing the nature of reality. I gathered that their philosophy professor had shaken them up. He asked them what reality was. He then rebutted each boy's answer. Hearing their story placed a question in my mind, *What is reality?*

Reality, in my mind, was to see and understand things as they are, have been, and will be. In other words, it is to have the Holy Spirit as a tutor. This definition would not have sufficed in the story of the boys and their professor. So, I placed the question of reality in the back of my mind.

Several weeks later while attending a devotional address by Virginia H. Pearce (see Pearce 1997), I revisited the question concerning the nature of reality as she spoke of the reality of the Holy Spirit speaking to us. Pondering during her address, I heard, "Reality is the state in which God exists."

Years later, I returned to her talk to quote her as a source, only to discover that she had not defined reality as the state in which God exists. It was the divine communicating with me.

Personal development books had a familiar ring to me. As I read, I feel the divine communicating with me. I noticed many of the universal principles taught were also found in scripture. For example, Dale Carnegie suggests that we ought to be "genuinely interested" in others. He also suggests the greatest word in the dictionary to anyone is his or her name. In my mind, he was giving application to the command that we should love one another as we love ourselves; thus, I use my divine, spiritual understanding to bring forth greater wisdom.

The following quote adds light to the topic,

> *Love is one of the chief characteristics of Deity, and ought to be manifested by those who aspire to be the sons of God. A man filled with the love of God, is not content with blessing his family alone, but ranges through the whole world, anxious to bless the whole human race (Smith 2007, 426).*

When we're genuinely interested in others, we want to learn from them and share what we know with them. This exchange of talents allows both parties to be edified and to rejoice together. (D&C 50:22).

Pure religion encompasses all truth. All truth—whether it be in math, science, humanities, history, etc.— leads to God. Indeed, "All things denote there is a God" (Alma 30:44).

I quote from the things I've read and studied. All things that lead us to do good, including personal development and churches, enhance our lives. A leader in my faith put it well:

> *Let me say that we appreciate the truth in all churches and the good which they do. We say to the people, in effect, you bring with you all the good that you have, and then let us see if we can add to it (Hinckley 1998, para. 5).*

This teaching is about learning from one another. It's about laying hold of every good thing that leads to Christ. He is the Way, the Truth, and the Light back to the Father (John 14:6).

When we study universal truths, we come to know Christ, who will lead us straight to our Father. The following quote demonstrates that Christ is the author of Truth,

> *Those who lay hold of the word of truth and trace it to its original source come to Christ. [Universal] truths are as the spokes of a wheel, all emanating from Christ who is the hub. Anyone who would accept and lay hold on these truths is automatically led to their author, Jesus Christ. (Caldwell 1992, para. 20).*

If all good leads to Christ, it becomes imperative that we learn how we fit in the "body of Christ" (1 Corinthians 12:27; Ephesians 4:12). We are all brothers and sisters. Let us work together in understanding God and in establishing His kingdom on earth as it is in heaven.

Before one begins teaching of God, however, one must know and live His word. It is written,

> *Seek not to declare my word, but first seek to obtain my word, and then shall your tongue be loosed; then, if you desire, you shall have my Spirit and my word, yea, the power of God unto the convincing of men. (D&C 11:21).*

When we obtain and live by the word of God, we are filled with His power.

Fleshy Tables

> *"The epistle of Christ ministered by us, written not with ink, but with the Spirit of the living God; not in tables of stone, but in fleshy tables of the heart" (2 Corinthians 3:3).*

Studying and writing a record of what we've received is not sufficient to become like our Master. We need to live by "every word that proceeds forth from the mouth of God" (Matthew 4:4). This word needs to be written on the "fleshy tables of [our] heart" (2 Cor. 3:3).

When God's word is written upon our hearts, we live it. We

become one with the Father. Our thoughts are in tune with His thoughts, and our ways are in harmony with His ways.

Living a Life on Fire is to know as you are known. It is to live in such a manner that those who know us know our Father in heaven.

In this chapter, we have discussed the **why** in seeking wisdom: seeking wisdom through the divine brings power of learning and an exchanging of light and truth. We have also learned that the greatest source for this knowledge is to gaze into heaven to see as God sees. Let us seek pure intelligence from "the Father of lights" (D&C 67:9).

In the following chapter, I refer to the bestselling book *Good to Great*. It teaches that all companies have access to the same information. However, some companies leap to greatness and others don't.

In the information age, we, like these companies, have access to a vast amount of knowledge. However, we must learn **how** to take the leap and access that knowledge. Taking the leap to holiness is about applying the knowledge received. Is it enough to be great?

CHAPTER 3

We've discussed the significance of gazing into heaven and seeing things as they really are. Studying all the books in the world will fall short of knowing God. Why not use the best books we study to open a conduit to higher knowledge?

This chapter discusses purifying our lives to live a Life on Fire. When we do, we can draw near to God.

Step 3: How?

"Good to Great" is Not Enough!

In Jim Collins' bestselling book, *Good to Great: Why Some Companies Make the Leap ... and Others Don't*, he teaches why some companies become great while others fall by the wayside. In this book, I'm exploring a similar notion but with a different point.

If I were to rewrite Collins' title, it would read *Good to Holy: Why Some Make the Leap ... and Others Don't*.

The only reason why individuals don't make the leap to holiness is the universal sin of pride. The following author sums up our failure to jump with two reasons:

1. the "fear of persecution"
2. "the cares of the world"

It may be one or the other or a combination of both. Read and reread the following loaded quote:

> *Just how effectively the devil can mount a two-front war against us is seen in the words of the Lord wherein he speaks of "the fear of persecution and the cares of the world" (D&C 40:2). If our appetites can be directed in such a way that we are caught up in the cares of the world, and if we are then also afraid of persecution because of doing what is right, we have been acted upon and are doubly deterred from discipleship. Some who might not fear persecution by itself do not choose to cope with the double load of persecution plus the cares of the world. Some for whom the cares of the world would not be sufficient to draw them away finally yield because of the fear of persecution. (Maxwell 1978, 91,)*

Recently, my wife brought to my attention something I told her in our first year of marriage. I told her that I watched two movies a week to keep me normal—to keep me from being "too good."

More than three years before I was married, I lived life to the fullest as I understood it. When I awoke in the State Hospital (for the mentally ill), I blamed part of my hospitalization on being "too good."

Almost 12 years into our marriage, she reminded me of what I had told her in our first year of marriage. She did this to pay me a compliment. It was about one month after being let go from my employment.

Termination from a job I enjoyed was a reality check. It was a call to action. A call to disregard the cares of the world and the fear of persecution. It was a call to "turn pro," as Steven Pressfield puts it in two of his nonfiction books, *The War of Art* and *Turning Pro*.

With the call to turn pro, I made some radical changes:

- I began going to bed earlier and getting up earlier.
- I began to sleep less than my previous average of 10 to 12 hours of sleep per day. (My average for about 15 years).
- I began working 12 hours or more per day.
- I began exercising regularly and losing weight.
- I began having more energy to engage with my family more.
- I began to live on purpose and with passion.
- I began living what I know and knowing more.
- I began having quantum leaps of faith.

After witnessing these changes, my dear wife was complimenting me for living on fire. She reminded me of the comment I made 12 years earlier about my fear of being too good. She then thanked me for living to the best of my abilities.

The adversary works to distract us and calls on our fears of persecution and cares of the world. One reason I slept so long was because of my lucid, grand dreams where I became a superhero saving the day or a basketball player dominating the court. With these grand dreams, I stayed asleep rather than facing my real dreams.

Everything clicked the day I was let go from my employment. I discovered that taking the quantum leap to turn pro doesn't take any more effort than being an amateur.

In Price Pritchett's book, *You2*, he defines what it takes to make a quantum leap. It is "mak[ing] 'jumps' without apparent effort and without covering all the bases between the starting and ending points" (2012, 4).

One may ask, what is the leap? It is to embrace your calling as if you could never fail at it.

You were given a calling from on High, and if you don't know it yet, it will come. Keep studying, keep searching, and keep asking. When you get it, it will come line upon line. The following quote explains the process:

A person may profit by noticing the first intimation of the spirit of revelation; for instance, when you feel pure intelligence flowing into you, it may give you sudden strokes of ideas, so that by noticing it, you may find it fulfilled the same day or soon; (i.e.) those things that were presented unto your minds by the Spirit of God, will come to pass; and thus by learning the Spirit of God and understanding it, you may grow into the principle of revelation, until you become perfect in Christ Jesus. (Smith 2007, 132).

Self-help and personal development books will teach you how to have the "Midas touch" or to have alchemy. For example, T. Harv Ecker says "Some people tell me I have the "Midas touch," where everything I get involved in turns to gold" (2009, 6).

However, what I am suggesting is more than just turning things into gold. Life is about tapping into the creative power itself. In Isaiah, we learn, "For my thoughts are not your thoughts, neither are your ways my ways, saith the Lord. For as the heavens are higher than the earth, so are my ways higher than your ways, and my thoughts than your thoughts" (Isaiah 55:8-9).

Isaiah is teaching us that, on our own, we cannot think God's thoughts, nor live his ways. However, in conjunction with the previous quote that "learning the Spirit of God and understanding it, you may grow into the principle of revelation, until you become perfect in Christ Jesus," it becomes clear that "in Christ" we can begin to comprehend God's thoughts and ways!

Thus, our purpose on earth is about more than mastering laws of success to turn things to gold. We're here to learn how to co-create with God, which includes all things working together for our good. Becoming one with Christ is essential in developing this power.

How do we do this?

It is by words ... [that] every being works when he works by faith. God said, 'Let there be light: and there was light.' Joshua spake, and the great lights which God had created stood still. Elijah commanded, and the heavens were stayed for the space of three years and six months, so that it did not rain. ... All this was done by faith. ... Faith, then, works by words; and with [words] its mightiest works have been, and will be, performed. (Holland 2007, para. 1)

Is it any wonder why we should 'live by every word that proceeds from the mouth of God?' Again turning to Isaiah, "So shall my word be that goeth forth out of my mouth: it shall not return unto me void, but it shall accomplish that which I please, and it shall prosper in the thing whereto I sent it" (Isaiah 55:11).

Learning the word of God, and living in harmony with it, will

41

bring about His fruits. It will empower us to become steadfast and immovable. His word will not return to us void, "for the word of God must be fulfilled" (Alma 5:58).

What am I suggesting? Both you and I ought to live the laws of success, discovering and acting on our unique calling without the fear of failure, not for the sake of being great, but for the sake of being holy.

In this chapter, we have discussed the **how** in seeking wisdom; we seek wisdom through finding and embracing our holy calling. In doing so, we must become one with Christ.

In the next chapter, we will discuss the **what to become**. All the what, why, and how of seeking wisdom leads to becoming holy. This is what we are to become: holy.

Chapter 4

We've discussed the first three steps in seeking wisdom:

- The 1st chapter is **what** we observe and do, even personal development;
- the 2nd chapter is **why** we reach for more; it is part of our spiritual DNA; and
- the 3rd chapter is **how** we achieve more, by making the leap to holiness through embracing our calling.

In this chapter, we will see **what to become**: become holy.

Step 4: What to become? Repeat!

Become Holy to Become One with God

Rather than serve the ego, we "become servants to God, [having our] fruit unto holiness" (Romans 6:22, bracket added).

We can grow into the principle of revelation "wax[ing] strong in the knowledge of the truth" even the knowledge of God by coming to "know" and live by "the word of God" (Alma 17:2).

Then "on account of [our] exceeding faith," having proven the word of God, we "are called with a holy calling" (Alma 13:3).

Being holy is a gift! Holiness is for those who do not "reject the Spirit of God on account of the hardness of their hearts and blindness of their minds" (Alma 13:4). To receive this gift, we must start with the word of God.

> *Like all gifts "which cometh from above," words are "sacred, and must be spoken with care, and by constraint of the Spirit." It is with this realization of the power and sanctity of words that I wish to caution us, if caution is needed, regarding how we speak to each other and how we speak of ourselves. (Holland 2007, para. 1-2)*

An imperative step on this journey of becoming one with the word of God unto holiness is to master our tongue. James teaches us how to be perfect. He wrote, "For in many things we offend all. If any man offend not in word, the same is a perfect man, and able also to bridle the whole body" (James 3:2).

How are we perfect? How do we bridle the whole body? By the proper use of our words!

James goes on to say "the tongue can no man tame" (James 3:8). It takes more than sheer will to tame our tongue. We have to yield to the enticing of the Holy Spirit, which will empower us to control our tongues. This is essential to obtaining holiness.

Holiness isn't about what you and I can or can't do with obedience to the laws of success. It's about what you and I can do when we tap into the Almighty word of God. Feasting upon His word will tell and show us what we are to say and do (2 Nephi 32:3, 5).

As we feast upon the word of God, we will receive instructions from on High. We will grow in His word line upon line, precept upon precept, here a little and there a little. This growth will continue until the perfect day when we comprehend all things (D&C 50:24; 88:67). We can say as did Christ, "The Son can do nothing of himself, but what he seeth the Father do: for what things soever he doeth, these also doeth the Son likewise" (John 5:19).

We do not receive of this fullness at once. We, like the Son of Man, have to grow in intelligence or the glory of God. We have to receive grace for grace, and grace to grace (see D&C 93:12-14).

We have two options:

1. we can learn and live the laws of success to become the richest man in Babylon; or
2. we can lay hold of every good thing and one day create worlds without number.

I choose the latter. I choose to be holy and become one with God.

Again this is not done in and of myself, for I am an "unworthy creature" (Mosiah 4:11). Holiness is "yielding" my life to the word of God that I may become "a saint" in Christ (Mosiah 3:19).

When we surrender our will to the Father's will, he makes more of us than we can of our own accord. In our limited foresight, we would accept a nice cottage or even a mansion to dwell in. But we're destined to be temples. C.S. Lewis sheds light on this process of turning our life over to the Lord:

Imagine yourself as a living house. God comes in to rebuild that house. At first, perhaps, you can understand what He is doing. He is getting the drains right and stopping the leaks in the roof and so on; you knew that those jobs needed doing and so you are not surprised. But presently He starts knocking the house about in a way that hurts abominably and does not seem to make any sense. What on earth is He up to? The explanation is that He is building quite a different house from the one you thought of - throwing out a new wing here, putting on an extra floor there, running up towers, making courtyards. You thought you were being made into a decent little cottage: but He is building a [temple]. He intends to come and live in it Himself. (1952, 205)

"He intends to come and live in" our temple, which He helped build. Remember when we "love [Christ], [we] will keep [His] words: and [God] will love [us], and [both God and His Son] will come unto [us], and make [Their] abode with [us] (John 14:23). This isn't a hyperbole. It's clear holy writ.

On another occasion, the Savior taught, "Behold, I stand at the door, and knock: if any man hear my voice and open the door, I will come in to him, and will sup with him, and he with me" (Revelation 3:20). Let us surrender to our Highest Power, even God the Father, and allow Him and His Son to sup with us.

This pivotal chapter has covered the paradigm shift needed to move to the world of holiness. Life isn't about being great, but about being holy. Holiness is power.

Now, that we have answered **what to become**—become holy—we are led to a new what, and we start the process again. Section 2 contains four chapters discussing the what, why, how, and what to become in seeking holiness.

SECTION 2

Seek Holiness

For what is a man profited, if he shall gain the whole world, and lose his own soul? or what shall a man give in exchange for his soul? For the Son of man shall come in the glory of his Father with his angels; and then he shall reward every man according to his works. (Matthew 16:26-27)

Success laws and principles will teach you how to gain wealth, health, and relationships. Imagine having more money than you can spend, being fit enough to live 150 years, and being famous, too. What would those three things do for you beyond the grave?

The moral of this section is that we must become more than success, we must become holy, even one with God. But how? We will answer this question in the next four chapters.

- First, we must seek the word of God, which must be *fulfilled.*
- Second, we will undergo a trial of our faith in the word.

- Third, we must view the trials of our faith as opportunities to prove God's word.
- And fourth, all three of the preceding steps take faith and lead to a more perfect eye of faith.

CHAPTER 5

Holiness is to live according to the word of God. As previously discussed, I could have become a McDonald's franchise owner. To do that would have been an accomplishment. Yet, Father had something else in store for me.

As children of the Most High, holiness is much more than acquiring what we desire in our finite minds. In this chapter, we'll discuss the ultimate source of holiness. It is to live in accordance with God's word.

After deciding to be holy or one with God, what must we do to take that leap of faith?

Step 1: What?

God's Word is Fulfilled

"The word of God must be fulfilled" (Alma 5:58).

To be holy, one must seek to know the word of God. Holy men and women who have preceded us in this mortal realm, have sought to be in harmony with His thoughts and ways. Holiness is salvation.

Gandhi gives an excellent explanation for salvation, when he describes

Moksha. In the introduction to his autobiography, he expresses his deepest yearning. He wrote, "What I want to achieve—what I have been striving and pining to achieve these thirty years—is self-realization, to see God face-to-face, to attain Moksha (salvation) (1993, xxvi).

Achieving salvation requires faith, even action. The Bible teaches, "Faith without works is dead" (James 2:20). It would be death to sit and be idle while dreaming of mansions above. We must, therefore, be engaged in righteous works to seek after holiness.

Christ taught, "Man shall not live by bread alone, but by every word that proceedeth out of the mouth of God" (Matthew 4:4). Bread is an important part of living, as is wealth, health, and relationships. But it's not the only thing we live by. The only way to achieve holiness is to know and live by the word of God.

Faith unto life and salvation

Study and read the following quote at least three times. Go the extra mile and memorize it. At least memorize the following three phrases from the quote: "the idea," "a correct idea," and "an actual knowledge."

Let us here observe, that three things are necessary in order that any rational and intelligent being may exercise faith in God unto life and salvation.

*First, **the idea** that he actually exists.*

*Secondly, **a correct idea** of his character, perfections, and attributes.*

*Thirdly, **an actual knowledge** that the course of life which he is pursuing is according to his will. For without*

*an acquaintance with these three important facts, the
faith of every rational being must be imperfect and
unproductive; but with this understanding it can become
perfect and fruitful, abounding in righteousness, unto the
praise and glory of God the Father, and the Lord Jesus
Christ. (Smith 1985, 38-39, emphasis added).*

Without knowing who God is, we would not seek to know His word. Without the correct idea of Him, we would not seek to be one with Him. With a correct idea of His character, perfections, and attributes, we seek to be holy like Him. We seek to align ourselves with His will.

Living by every word that proceeds from the mouth of God allows us to become "perfect and fruitful." We cannot merely guess what His word is, and while believing in His word is a start, it still isn't good enough. We need "an actual knowledge" that our "course" is in line with "His will."

You could sign up to work for the adversary and receive his wages. The adversary can offer wealth, fame, and worldly power in exchange for doing his dirty deeds. But what will this do for you in the eternities? Nothing he offers has value. There is no divine currency, nor holiness, in unrighteousness. Neal A. Maxwell, a modern-day apostle of Jesus Christ, expressed this imagery more eloquently:

*How tragic it is that so many mortals are mercenaries for
the adversary; that is, they do his bidding and are hired by
him—bought off at such low prices. A little status, a little
money, a little praise, a little fleeting fame, and they are
willing to do the bidding of him who can offer all sorts of
transitory "rewards," but who has no [divine] currency. It
is amazing how well the adversary has done; his
mercenaries never seem to discover the self-destructive*

nature of their pay and the awful bankruptcy of their poor paymaster! (1978, 42)

God's word must be fulfilled, and it offers eternal lives, even all that He has. Let us therefore seek to know what His word is that we may be holy like unto Him. Remember, Holiness is His name!

In this chapter, we learned **what** we are to seek—God's word. As we obtain the word of God, we will be blessed with trials to prove our hearts and minds. Will we live by His word?

God already knows the outcome. The trial is an opportunity for you to prove your beliefs. This proving ground allows you to turn belief into actual knowledge.

For example, a child may plant a seed and nurture it. But until she sees it sprout for the first time, it's not knowledge. Likewise, until our belief and faith are tried, we cannot know. In the following chapter, I will share an intimate story of my faith being tried in order to show **why** we need to seek God's word and thereby seek holiness.

Chapter 6

In the last chapter, we covered the power of God's word being fulfilled. If we desire to be holy, we must live in harmony with God's word. Living according to His word is more than a hunch, but an actual knowledge.

In this chapter, I share a personal story of how my faith was tried by facing my greatest fear.

Step 2: Why?

Trial of Thy Faith

"Faith is things which are hoped for and not seen; wherefore, dispute not because ye see not, for ye receive no witness until after the trial of your faith" (Ether 12:6).

A more proper title for this chapter should be Trial of *My* Faith. I am about to share a grand and personal trial of my faith. It is my hope that you can liken this unto yourself, and my story can serve as a catalyst, empowering you to be wiser than I.

Shortly upon my return from Outer Mongolia, where I served as a voluntary missionary for two years, I visited a close friend in the Utah State Hospital for the mentally ill. My friend was being treated for a nervous breakdown.

While visiting this friend, we discussed some of the basic truths that I had been teaching in Mongolia. He had served a mission too but had forgotten many of these basic truths.

Worrying that mental illness was heredity, I knew I could fall victim as my family had a strong history of it. Deep down, this had always been my greatest fear.

As I visited him in one of his moments of trial, I made a childish vow that I would never let that happen to me. I then began deducing how I could avoid mental illness. My two deductions proved to be incorrect.

First, I thought that part of his plight was the result of disobedience to what he knew to be true. Second, I thought that if he had never taken worldly medicine, he would have never needed them. With both of those false premises in mind, I committed to remain faithful and to never take medicine.

With earnest zeal, I set about to prove these notions true.

Five years almost to the day, I awoke in the same hospital. I had been court ordered to the State Hospital for 6 months. Schizoaffective: bipolar type was my diagnosis.

In a baffled state, I spent the next three years trying to figure out what had happened to me. It didn't make sense. I had kept every jot and tittle to the best of my knowledge:

I magnified my callings.

I served and loved others.

I went to school.

I ran for office in student government.

I dated Heavenly Father's choice daughters.

I attended the temple.

I studied the word, etc.

I was so set on doing everything right. My pursuit was for perfection in Christ. In retrospect, I was blind to my overzealous and fanatical nature.

The adversary utilized my fear against me. I was plagued with the idea of avoiding mental illness. This plague only expedited my nervous breakdown.

I was in my mid-20s and full of life. But my life came crashing down around me. One early morning, I turned to priesthood leaders for a blessing. The night before I called for this blessing, I broke up with my fiancée.

On the call, I explained that my hands were cold. My false logic was that cold hands meant one had lost the authority to exercise priesthood power.

When the ecclesiastical leaders came and offered a blessing of healing rather than of comfort, I was stunned. I did not understand why I needed a blessing of healing. I felt fine; I just wanted to move forward with being made perfect in Christ. Something, unbeknown to me, was amiss.

Within a week, while walking home from Brigham Young University (BYU) campus, I saw a pillar of light. This light descended from high in the sky. But before it reached me, I closed my eyes as if I were blind.

Not wanting to make a scene on campus, I stood there as if I were blind. Within moments, a young man approached me and asked if I needed any help. I told him I could not see, and I would love an escort home. With my instructions, he directed me to my home near campus.

When we arrived at my door, I asked him to knock three times, and I believed I would be able to see again. He knocked, I opened my eyes, and I walked in my home.

In retrospect, I don't understand why I did what I did. It doesn't make sense, but this is an excellent example of how something was amiss in my thinking.

A day or two later, two psychologists, escorted by two or three police officers, came to my home. They visited with me and suggested I come to the Regional hospital to be evaluated.

I was in shock. Me go to the hospital? I didn't want to go, and I was a bit perturbed that they walked in without someone answering the door. So, I asked them if I could call my lawyer. I made the call, thinking I had caught them in some wrongdoing such as unlawful entry. But, to my surprise, I didn't catch anything but an invitation to follow their instructions. AAAHH, off to the hospital!

On the way to the hospital, in the police car, I started to cry as I received a false revelation. With that revelation, I thought Christ's church and the hospital were in cahoots. I thought the purpose of me going to the hospital was twofold. One, to be sealed to a girl I wasn't dating, and two, to receive my calling and election. This false revelation touched my soul.

After scrutinizing the admittance papers, I signed them. While waiting in the emergency room, I gave every detail of my prior hospitalizations. Again, I thought this was part of the process needed to receive holy ordinances.

Then some security guards came to escort me with a nurse. Reality hit me when I discovered we weren't going to a secret room, but to the psych ward. I then asked them to turn around, which they refused. With my false logic, I thought since I had signed that I would come in of my own free will, I could leave now of my own free will.

When they would not turn around, I stood to my feet and started to walk out. The guards stepped in and tried to wrestle me down. Because I was strong in stature, they could not do it. Then a female nurse got down between their legs and grabbed my legs to trip me. Not desiring to hurt or strike anyone, I let her trip me, and I fell to my knees. I was then strapped down and given a sedative. (Voluntary status became involuntary admission).

Still holding on to my belief that medicine was not of God, I refused to take the medicine offered. Finally, after about a week, I spoke with the same lawyer friend. He invited me to take the medicine, and I did. Shortly thereafter, I went home.

Less than two weeks later, I was arrested for trespassing on Temple Square. Here's what happened, beginning with some backdrop:

I refused to take more medicine. So the only medicine I took was in the hospital. Remember, I believed addiction to medicine was a culprit to mental illness.

I volunteered at the Missionary Training Center (MTC). I would translate things in English to Mongolian for the Mongolian missionaries. I became friends with a senior couple serving there.

One day, I discussed some of my ideas about having a calling and election made sure with this senior couple. They had a genuine interest. When I asked them some questions, they suggested I speak with the MTC president. I felt honored with such a notion. So, I did.

They then made a phone call, and within moments, I was meeting with the MTC president. With grace, he brought me to his office and explained that it was Wednesday, one of his busiest days at the MTC. Every Wednesday, a huge new group of missionaries come to the MTC. As a result, he did not have time to discuss my questions. Rather he offered me a phone number to speak with a general authority (a high leader in my worldwide faith). AMAZING, I thought.

Rather than call, I decided to go the extra mile and drive to my faith's headquarters. I could be there in about an hour.

On the way there, I had racing thoughts; I was so excited to meet a general authority. I thought the phone number given was a pass to talk to a general authority.

I also had the idea that I was coming to save the day on a white horse. This idea was so strong that I contemplated borrowing a friend's white car, rather than my navy blue car. But I dismissed this idea due to the time crunch. It would be past 5 PM if I did that, and I would miss my opportunity to speak with a general authority that day. (The thought did not occur to me that I could go up the next day; it was urgent, I had to seize the day).

As the thoughts continued to race, I devised a plan for my arrival. I went straight to a security guard and told him my intentions to see a general authority. And I told him my master plan, devised to show and prove my worthiness, so I would then be allowed to approach a general authority to discuss my calling and election.

I intended to go to the temple, present my recommendation, and prove that I was worthy to be on temple grounds while dressed in casual clothes (rather than the customary suit and tie).

Then I was going to race to the Church office building before 5 PM to speak with a general authority. I explained that I had their phone number, and I decided to visit in person instead.

He advised me to not proceed. But I pressed forward to go the extra mile to visit with a general authority.

On my way to check in at the temple desk, I ran into a friend who was now serving at temple square as a voluntary missionary. She advised me to go take my medicine. This baffled me. I don't need medicine, I thought. Then in an attempt to comfort me, she explained that she took medicine and that I ought to take some medicine too.

I brushed off her counsel, and pointing to her name badge, I spouted off something like, "you don't have to be a missionary to carry His name." I then proceeded with my plan to go to the sentinels at the entrance of the temple and present my recommendation. After leaving, I headed toward the church office building.

Just as I passed the threshold of the temple fence, a security guard asked me if he could ask me some questions. I agreed, not thinking of the time (close to 5 PM). He asked what I was doing there; I repeated what I had told the first security guard. He then asked me a peculiar question. He asked if I wanted to see the prophet (aka president of the Church). I couldn't believe it. I told him I would love to see the prophet. He then advised me to call it a day, and informed me that everyone was getting ready to go home. I looked at the time and thought, I can still make it if I hurry, and I explained this to him. After some exchange, he asked me if I would like to pray in the grass by the temple. I thought this odd, but I agreed to his invitation.

As we approached, I asked if this was a good spot. He said a bit closer. Once we were where he wanted us to be, I dropped to my knees. Under normal circumstances, I would not have offered a prayer on my knees in the middle of Temple Square.

Before I could utter two sentences, two police officers picked me up and escorted me off temple square. Each of them held me above their shoulders by an armpit. What was happening? I was there to talk to a general authority about calling and elections. Now these two officers were forcing me off Temple Square. I felt violated. When I asked their names, one said, "My name is Joseph," and the other said, "My name is Smith" and they laughed. Then, outside of the gates of Temple Square, they shoved my face in the flowerbed dirt and handcuffed me. To this day, I still have a scar from the handcuffs.

[As a side bar: I have nothing against police officers, and I forgave them. They didn't know any better. It's obvious that they were not trained CIT (Crisis Intervention Training) officers. I'm sure everyone was following protocol, and I'm grateful for the arrest. It led to me getting help.]

I later found out the arrest was for trespassing. Charges were dropped, but my story wasn't over. I don't know how long I was in jail. Suffice it to say, about two weeks later, I woke up in the State Hospital.

Before I woke up, I was coherent enough to refuse medicine. But I didn't know where I was or what I was doing. I do remember wearing a blanket over my head as if I were a disciple of Christ 2000 years ago. I have fragmented memories of the staff feeding and showering me. And I remember some of the security guards pinning me to the ground. While I was down, the doctors stuck a needle in my behind to medicate me.

After being medicated, I woke up! I recognized where I was. I was in the exact place—the State Hospital—I had visited my friend 5 years before. I couldn't believe it. How did I get there? What had become of me? You mean this medicine helped me? You mean these doctors are here to help me? It's not me against the world?

While in the state hospital, I had earned the highest privileges. I could roam about the campus. I could check out books from the library and go to the cafeteria. Within less than 6 weeks total, I was in a halfway house.

A month later, I moved out on my own, got a job at McDonald's, and went back to school to take a summer class at BYU. The following fall I enrolled full time.

With lack of energy, continued weight gain, and facing the reality of being mentally ill, I fell into depression. This led to being overwhelmed with my latest major change to philosophy (it was about my ninth declared major for my undergraduate work). As a result, I withdrew from school to give myself some time to figure out what to do with my life.

Just months before, I was on my A game. I was about to marry a beautiful girl from a great family. I had a nice car. I had an 8-pack washboard for a stomach. And I thought I was popular.

Almost overnight, I lost everything. I was no longer engaged. I was gaining weight. (I ended up gaining 60 pounds in 9 months). I was working at McDonald's making $7.50 an hour. No one outside of my parents and the ecclesiastical leaders came to visit me while I was in the State hospital. And my car was impounded and sold while I was in the hospital.

Confusion befuddled me. Searching for meaning, I sunk into despair. I didn't comprehend how this could have happened to me when I had lived my life to the best of my knowledge.

My mission president comforted me. He was in remission from cancer and encouraged me to press forward. I did. But still I had unanswered questions.

I moved to SLC with a friend from high school. I landed a job as a courier, which gave me the freedom to do some soul searching. I was sleeping about 12 hours a day. I listened to audio books from the library while driving. I went on a few dates and did a lot of praying.

Facing mental illness was my trial of faith like that of Job. Like Job, I lost everything that I thought was important:

> My fiancée. (I broke up with her.)

> My physique. (I gained weight as side effect of medicine.)

> My popularity and friends. (None of them visited me or stayed connected, with the exception of my roommate.)

> My car. (Impounded and sold before I got out of the hospital.)

> My major in college. (Philosophy became too taxing, and I withdrew from school.)

Nevertheless, with the loss of all these things, I proceeded to follow the leaders of my faith. I couldn't forget my covenant to the Lord. Yet, having lived a righteous life, how could I have mental illness?

Despite my questions of "why me?" and "how could this be?" I continued to read the word of God, study the best books, pray, attend church, magnify callings, and write in a journal. For months and months, even years, I sought for the answers. How could I bear such things? This was a trial of my faith.

> *And now, I, Moroni, would speak somewhat concerning these things; I would show unto the world that faith is things which are hoped for and not seen; wherefore, dispute not because ye see not, for ye receive no witness until after the trial of your faith. (Ether 12:6)*

What kept me going? Hope.

> *Wherefore, whoso believeth in God might with surety hope for a better world, yea, even a place at the right hand of God, which hope cometh of faith, maketh an anchor to the souls of men, which would make them sure and steadfast, always abounding in good works, being led to glorify God (Ether 12:4).*

From previous experience, I also knew that Father knew what I needed. I knew that I had to have hope in Him and not expect what I wanted (see Proverbs 10:28-29). Thus, I went about living the best of what I knew.

But I still wanted to know why me. Then an answer came in my studying of the word. I came upon a quote by Elder Neal A. Maxwell that altered the course of my life. It read, "So often the invitation to greater consecration comes by means of painful, personal experiences" (1995, 15).

This quote reminded me of a paradigm shift I had in my 18th year. When I read that I was raised in a manner to prepare me for righteousness,

I drew back. I was raised in a furnace of affliction, and it was a blessing? To this question, I received a "yes" answer. I learned that because of my struggles, I had greater empathy and love.

Now in retrospect of Maxwell's quote, I learned:

- Living a righteous life does not prevent you from experiencing trial and tribulation.
- Mental illness, like rain, falls upon the righteous and wicked.
- Proper use of medicine is a powerful source for healing (it saved my life).
- Praise be to the mental institutions that work to help the mentally ill, not to punish them.
- Praise be to modern medicine that helps our brains to function more wholly.
- Trials of our faith are lessons of humility (see Ether 12:27, 37). And they teach us how dependent upon the Lord we are.
- Gratitude that being thus compelled, I sought repentance (see Alma 32:13).
- To have greater empathy and compassion.
- Father, knowing what I needed, prepared an individual plan of happiness for me.
- That my "painful personal experience" was a gift from Father.
- And that my perceived weakness could become a strength with the Grace of Christ (Ether 12:27).

In short, trials—even painful personal experiences—are but an invitation to greater consecration. Father has an individual plan of happiness designed for each of us. His plan will draw us nearer to Him. Trials of faith strengthen, not weaken, our faith.

Trials and tribulations help us remember God that we may live by every word that proceeds from His mouth. As a perfected being, He knows what we need to receive perfection. If He blessed us without trying our faith, we could forget Him and be filled with pride (see Helaman 12:2-3).

Thank you for allowing me to share an intimate and personal story of growth in my life.

This trying experience compelled me to humility (Alma 32:13). With Elder Maxwell's quote, I learned that my "painful personal experience" was not a punishment; rather, it was part of a divine plan of a wise Father who knew what I needed in order to come closer to Him.

Trials are designed to prove our hearts. This trial helped turn my belief to actual knowledge. I was on the path to "greater consecration," even the path of holiness.

To turn our beliefs into actual knowledge, our faith will be tried. These trials and afflictions are blessings. They draw us closer to the Lord and give us the opportunity to prove His word in our lives.

Rather than fight a trial, lean into it by continuing to live His word. Embracing your trial with faith in Christ will enable quantum leaps in your life. These leaps will help you ask the right questions. As suggested earlier, when you ask inspired questions, you will receive answers and power from on High.

Chapter 5 covered the **what** of God's word being fulfilled. In this last chapter, I shared **why** embracing my trial with faith (or continuing to live God's word) lead to greater holiness. In the next chapter, we'll discuss **how** we prove God's word or how to know His word.

CHAPTER 7

In this chapter, we will discuss how God's word is fulfilled in our lives. We know that God's word must be fulfilled, and we will undergo a trial of our faith to test our faithfulness to God's word. Living the reality of these first two steps is but an opportunity to prove God's words.

Step 3: How?

Prove the Word of God

"By Faith all things are fulfilled" (Ether 12:3).

Many talk of life being a test from God. It's a test to see if we would be holy like Him or not. God knows the beginning from the end. As such, He knows the results of the exam. Do you?

The only way to know the results of the exam is to prove the word of God in our lives. This proving could be likened unto the scientific approach.

Rather than make a hypothesis from our own thinking, we ought to seek to know God's word from holy men and women. Then we must prove their words. Are these words of God or are they words of a mortal man? (see John 7:17).

How do we prove the word of God others have spoken? We start with belief in the word of God shared with us. Just as the child planted her first seed earlier, we need to plant the seed of the word of God in our hearts.

As we continue to water the seed by laying hold of every good thing and feed it with the best books, our bosoms swell with fire and the seed will begin to sprout with action. Remember to be patient and allow a time of gestation. If there is no fire, no growth, no raised awareness for good and no results in increased godliness, you will know that it's not a good seed and it will fall by the wayside (see D&C 9:8-9).

As we continue to nourish the sprout with more light and truth, it will grow filling us with joy. But there is more to nurturing the seed than planting in good ground. We must also hedge up the edges by praying always to come off conquering the adversary and his minions (D&C 10:5).

Moving forward requires more than belief. It takes faith. Faith is to act in accordance with the seed (word, law, principle) you have planted. When we do this, we tap into God's power. And like an acorn seed, all the nutrients needed for growth will come together for your good.

What would you do if you knew you could not fail? By living the word of God through faith in Christ, we cannot fail! Partaking of His fruit endows us with spiritual gifts and powers. Gifts such as charity never fail, and with God's power, we can become immovable.

The only way one can control the powers of heaven is to be governed by righteous principles. Being governed by His word includes looking unto Him with every thought. (see D&C 121:36; 88:34; and 6:36).

How do we watch our thoughts? What do we fill the thought stage of our minds with moment to moment? The following quote expounds upon the controlling of our thoughts,

Your mind is like a stage in a theater; in the theater of your mind, however, only one actor can be on stage at a time. If the stage is left bare, thoughts of darkness and sin often enter the stage to tempt. But these thoughts have no power if the stage of your mind is occupied by wholesome thoughts, such as a memorized hymn or verse of scripture that you can call upon in a moment of temptation. By controlling the stage of your mind, you can successfully resist persistent urges to yield to temptation and indulge in sin. You can become pure and virtuous. (LDS 2004, 119, emphasis added).

We must let virtue garnish the thought stage of our spiritual mind's eye (D&C 121:45). By guarding our thoughts, we can conquer what we think about and have holy thoughts.

Holy thoughts give us power to control our tongue. As referred to earlier, he who controls his words => controls his body => and is a perfect man (James 3:2).

The word is plain. We are the managers of the thought stage of our mind. Let us prove this word of God by choosing what we allow on our thought stage. Watching our thoughts will empower us to control our tongue, body, and environment. Remember the words of King Benjamin, we are to watch our thoughts, words, and deeds, that we perish not (Mosiah 4:30).

Before we can prove God's word, we have to learn it. As we learn it, we will be tried to see if we will adhere to it. This trial is a proving ground for our hearts to be purged of what is unholy.

As our thoughts are purified, we learn **how** to seek holiness: proving God's words by living them. When we live God's words in our lives, we come to an actual knowledge that we are living according to His will. Doing so will enlarge our vision of possibilities. As we do this, we see **what we are to become**: someone who sees with the eye of faith. Living the Word of God opens the window for us to see with an "eye of faith."

CHAPTER 8

Knowing and living the word of God gives us the power of godliness. With this power, we become agents of righteous faith. We begin to see more clearly how things are, have been, and will be. With this vision, comes enhanced faith, even an eye of faith.

Step 4: What to become? Repeat!

An Eye of Faith

And there were many whose faith was so exceedingly strong, even before Christ came, who could not be kept from within the veil, but truly saw with their eyes the things which they had beheld with an eye of faith, and they were glad. (Ether 12:19).

And thus, if ye will not nourish the word, looking forward with an eye of faith to the fruit thereof, ye can never pluck of the fruit of the tree of life. (Alma 32:40).

We are to become holy men and women. To do this, we need to find holy men and women to follow.

When someone has been kind to you and shown you mercy, you feel of God's love. There is a reason why people do what they do. When you come across an example of God's love, ask them for a reason of their hope. Remember inquiry precedes revelation and understanding.

One of the quickest ways to learn the correct character of holiness is to turn to the scriptures. In the scriptures, you'll discover holy men and women. By following their example as a prototype, we'll come to know Deity.

Holy individuals or couples should not be placed on an unreachable pedestal, nor should they be worshiped. We may revere their works, but if we really revered their works, we would emulate them. Likewise, prophets and prophetesses are praiseworthy, and they teach a pattern for us to follow. Soak in this next quote, read it more than once,

> Prophets, those with the spirit of prophecy and revelation, are but the pattern; they are but illustrations or examples of what all the children of the Father are expected to be. Whatever spiritual endowment they have received, all are entitled to receive. The manner in which God converses with them is but the prototype of the manner in which God will converse with each of his children. (McConkie 1988, 188).

We're destined to be more than great; we're to be holy! Like unto the prophets of old and present, we have access to the same power and authority based upon our righteous living.

Having an eye of faith is to hold a model of righteousness in our mind's eye. We must behold the fruits of righteousness in our mind's eye. We must see ourselves partaking of the fruit of the seed we plant in our hearts.

As we think on those that are good and emulate their works, we will see changes in our feelings and our environment. We will then seek to multiply those works and partake of similar fruits. In time, the seeds of righteousness will grow into a mighty tree that will bear fruits, allowing others to partake.

The beauty is "no man is an island." When you change your fruits by planting a righteous seed (the word of God), you'll begin to bear fruits that others can partake of. In so doing, the one seed can become a forest filled with righteous trees.

Like begets like. Partake of the good works done to you and do likewise, so that you may promote holiness. Live your life in such a manner that others may know Deity by knowing you. And in so doing, you will discover your divine nature and live it to the fullest.

This second section has covered four chapters that show how God's word is fulfilled in each of us. Here's a synopsis of the four chapter in this section:

1. **What** we must do: seek and follow God's word as it must be fulfilled.

2. **Why** we need to seek God's word: so we can be tried to see if we will live His word or not.

3. Living by faith, according to the word of God, is **how we** turn our faith into an actual knowledge. Remember by faith all things are fulfilled, including God's word.

4. With this actual knowledge, our eye of faith increases.

Thus, we know **what to become**: someone living our divine nature to the fullest.

In the next chapter, we'll learn how to plant that seed and allow it to grow from the angle of a farmer rather than a child planting a seed in a cup. As children, we planted the one seed to see if it really would grow.

With our seed of wisdom planted in section one, and with the nurturing of that seed by seeking God's word for fulfillment where a sprout came forth from our trials, we are now ready for the next section, which will discuss the sprout becoming a tree.

SECTION 3

We have covered two sections up to this point. The first section explained **what** we are to seek—wisdom. The second sections told us **why** we seek it—for holiness. In this third section, we will see **how** we obtain it—by receiving the divine nature.

Seek the divine nature

Grace and peace be multiplied unto you through the knowledge of God, and of Jesus our Lord, According as his divine power hath given unto us all things that pertain unto life and godliness, through the knowledge of him that hath called us to glory and virtue: Whereby are given unto us exceeding great and precious promises: that by these ye might be partakers of the divine nature, having escaped the corruption that is in the world through lust. (2 Peter 1:2-4)

Have you spent years of your life working to comprehend and adhere to universal truths? If so, you've seen and received many blessings in your life. Yet, in longing for more, perhaps you've read the following: "Many are called but few are chosen" (Matthew 22:14) and wondered what you had to do to be chosen.

If you are one who is built upon good ground, you are one who is honest and has a good heart. You are one who hears and implements the good you know and, as such, you bring forth good fruits (see Luke 8:15). If the preceding two sentences describe you, you are chosen!

A few years ago, I received some flattering mail. It told me that I was being watched from afar and that my good works were known. It then taught me that if I would purchase a book, which lead to buying several books, I would learn how to become rich and famous.

Seeking for an outer confirmation that I was chosen, I purchased the books. But I found the material and the letters from this organization to be missing the *mark*. However good the flattery felt, something was amiss.

Sometime later, I came upon the following quote: "We can sometimes waste years of our lives waiting to be chosen (see D&C 121:34–36). But that is a false premise. You are already chosen" (Uchtdorf 2014, 4).

What a quote! These words empowered me to realize I didn't need flattery to know that I was chosen. I knew that I was chosen because I was following my Master as taught in Luke 8:15.

When we accept and lay hold of every good thing, we are among the chosen. And, the ultimate sign of this calling is to partake of the divine nature.

Our carnal mind and flesh will oppose this inkling to partake of the divine nature. Why does it oppose? Why is there resistance? Because by partaking of the divine nature, it is certain death to the carnal or natural man. I love this following scripture,

For the natural man is an enemy to God, and has been from the fall of Adam, and will be, forever and ever, unless he yields to the enticings of the Holy Spirit, and putteth off the natural man and becometh a saint through the atonement of Christ the Lord, and becometh as a child, submissive, meek, humble, patient, full of love, willing to submit to all things which the Lord seeth fit to inflict upon him, even as a child doth submit to his father. (Mosiah 3:19)

The carnal mind will oppose your desire to partake of the divine nature. But with humility and yielding to the Holy Spirit that invites you to do good continually, you will conquer it.

The divine nature frees you from being acted upon, and allows you to act for yourself. It empowers you to be an agent for Christ. Being an agent for Christ is to lay hold of every good thing. It is to adhere or cleave unto light and truth as it comes your way.

Literally as you partake of the fruits of the Spirit and hearken to its promptings, you are like the child who submits willingly to his father. And as you submit to those fruits, you will be filled with the divine nature.

CHAPTER 9

When we adhere to the word of God, we are laying hold of every good thing. This process of receiving more and more light and truth dispels darkness from us.

Each of us has two natures, a carnal nature and a divine nature. By laying hold of every good thing, we are saying goodbye to the carnal nature. This process of conversion is the same as when you turn a light on in a dark room—there is no more darkness (D&C 88:67).

As you receive wisdom and move forward to holiness, you become a saint. This is done by receiving the divine nature—a nature that will forsake the carnal nature.

Step 1: What?

Conversion = Saintliness

"To convert is to change from one status to another, and gospel conversion consists in the transformation of man from his fallen and carnal state to a state of saintliness" (McConkie 1965, 770).

Earlier, I suggested Reality is a state in which God exists. Yielding to the enticing of the Holy Spirit is to hear something good and do likewise. This will draw us closer to Reality, and we'll begin to see things as they really are, as they really have been, and as they really will be (see Jacob 4:13). Living in this manner is what it is to be a saint. Noah Webster defined a saint as, "A person sanctified; a holy or godly person; one eminent for piety and virtue. It is particularly applied to the apostles and other holy persons mentioned in Scripture" (Webster 2014, 62).

Conversion begins when we lay hold of good things and live accordingly. This could take years of toil or it could happen in an instant.

In the New Testament, we learn of a man's life changing with an experience. Saul went about persecuting the saints, until the Lord appeared to him and asked why. Saul then asked, "the greatest question you can ask in this world, Lord, what wilt thou have me to do?" (Benson 1984, para. 23). And the beauty of Saul, who became Paul, was that he "persisted in asking of that simple eight-word question" for the remainder of his life (Benson 1984, para. 23).

This quantum leap of conversion does not take years or any greater effort. But it does take courage and action. When we continue to ask the same question as Saul *and* follow the response, we will take the leap of faith to catapult us to conversion.

The following quote explains what a quantum leap is and the effort needed to take it,

Fred Alan Wolf, in his award-winning book titled Taking the Quantum Leap, describes the term as: "... the explosive jump that a particle of matter undergoes in

moving from one place to another ... in a figurative sense, taking the quantum leap means taking a risk, going off into an uncharted territory with no guide to follow." Physicists studying quantum mechanics note that particles make these "jumps" without apparent effort and without covering all the bases between the starting and ending points. (Pritchett 2012, 4)

The only thing I would correct about this quote is that we do have a guide in taking this quantum leap of conversion. Our guide is the light of Christ or our conscience. It is a light within us where we know right from wrong, and as we continue to cleave to or yield to these nudges for good, we are filled with more and more light and truth.

Yielding to this spiritual guide from within is key to the power of saintliness and it will lead you to greater spiritual gifts, including the gift of the Holy Ghost. This latter gift is the gift by which "[we] may know the truth of all things" (Moroni 10:5).

The Holy Ghost is a member of the Godhead. As such, He "comprehends more than all the world; and [we ought to] associate [ourselves] with him" (Smith 2007, 132).

In this chapter, we have learned **what** it means to be a saint. Saintliness is the product of choosing good over evil in all that you do and say. It's the purging of our thoughts from all that is not holy. It's being a recipient of the divine nature and forsaking the carnal nature. Partaking of the divine nature is a gift from God.

In the following chapter, we will see the significance of thinking higher thoughts which teaches us **why** we need to seek saintliness. Our finite minds would be happy with creating skyscrapers whereas higher thoughts think of creating worlds.

CHAPTER 10

In the previous chapter, we saw that conversion is jumping from carnal thinking to divine thinking. This jump is necessary to lift our thoughts to a higher plan to move them from alchemy to creation. Having the Midas touch pales in comparison to creating worlds without number. In this chapter, we see how finite our thoughts are.

Step 2: Why?

Our ways and thoughts ≠ God's Ways and Thoughts (but they can)

For my thoughts are not your thoughts, neither are your ways my ways, saith the Lord. For as the heavens are higher than the earth, so are my ways higher than your ways, and my thoughts than your thoughts. (Isaiah 55:8-9).

In the times of the tower Babel, all of God's children were "one." It is written, "And the Lord said, Behold, the people is one, and they have all one language; and this they begin to do: and now nothing will be restrained from them, which they have imagined to do" (Genesis 11:6).

When the people are "one," nothing will be restrained from them; they will do that which they imagine to do. So, what did they imagine to do? They wanted to build a tower to heaven, thinking it would lead them to eternal life.

Knowing what we know about space travel, it would be absurd to build a large building to reach God's home. Nevertheless, we as mortals could be pleased with the creation of a beautiful city lined with skyscrapers.

Rather than build a physical building, which will rust and decay over hundreds of years, we have the privilege to build a holy temple unto the Lord with the lives we live. We have the possibilities to create something that will last through eternity, even our character and the attributes of godliness.

Our thoughts and ways are not God's thoughts and ways, but they can be! As previously mentioned, the "paramount personal question" we ought to be asking is best described in the following quote,

> Paul asked a simple eight-word question—and the persistent asking of the same question changed his life. "Lord, what wilt thou have me to do?" (Acts 9:6.) The persistent asking of that same question can also change your life. There is no greater question that you can ask in this world. (Benson 1984, para. 23).

Like Saul, who first asked this question and later became Paul through following the reply, we too can change. Those who hear the good word and hearken to it are those of whom the Lord spoke in his parable of the seed falling on good ground (Luke 8:15). Thus, the change comes from not only hearing the reply to the greatest question leading to change, but in hearkening to it.

When we are converted, our thoughts and ways may become like unto our Father's thoughts and ways. And the only way to do that is to become one with Christ through His atonement. Which is done by "lay[ing] hold of every good thing" (Moroni 7:19). As mentioned earlier, when we lay hold of universal truths, we are led to Christ. For He is the author of all good. He is "the way, the truth, and the life" and "no man cometh" to know the thoughts and ways of "the Father, but by [Christ]" (John 14:6).

To convert from our Saul-like natures, we too ought to ask the Lord, "What wilt thou have me to do?" (Acts 9:6). This question opens the conduit to further light and truth, and there is no end to this growth.

In this chapter, we have discovered **why** it is important to think higher thoughts: to align our thoughts and ways with our Father, to become one with Christ.

In the next chapter, we will discuss **how** we do this by desiring increase rather than saying we have enough.

CHAPTER 11

In the previous chapter, we discussed the significance of being happy with building a skyscraper, versus creating worlds without number. Once we start on the path to holiness, we are promised growth in intelligence until we receive all that the Father has. Saying we have enough with a skyscraper is finite.

This chapter will discuss being recipients of the infinite. The key to opening this door is to never say, "I have enough," but to thirst after righteousness forevermore.

Step 3: How?

Never Say I have Enough

When we say we have enough, we lose what we have been given. This notion is explained well in the parable of the talents. The servant who hid his talent in fear of losing it had that which was given him taken away (see Matthew 25:14-30). This is like saying I have enough.

The following scripture and commentary expose the significance of never saying I have enough.

For behold, thus saith the Lord God: I will give unto the children of men line upon line, precept upon precept, here a little and there a little; and blessed are those who hearken unto my precepts, and lend an ear unto my counsel, for they shall learn wisdom; for unto him that receiveth I will give more; and from them that shall say, We have enough, from them shall be taken away even that which they have. (2 Nephi 28:30)

This holy writ suggests that which is given shall be taken away if we say we have enough. I know of many people who learn of God's word, and it changes their lives. Then after a time, they stop growing. And they begin to lose the changes they had made.

The Savior spoke of this in Luke Chapter 11. He teaches that is better for a person to not know good than it is to know good and then not hearken to it. He tells the story of a man who is changed, cleans his home, and then ends up in worse situation than before (see Luke 11:24-26).

The solution to permanent change is to live what you know and to know more—growth. It's to establish divine habits and routines. It's about developing divine attributes and living with the power of godliness.

To never say, "I have enough" is to receive more and more until we comprehend all things. This comprehension is no less than to see as we are seen, to know as we are known. It's to be on the path of mastery leading to Reality—the state in which God exists.

To see things as they really are, have been, and will be is to see in "one eternal round" (D&C 35:1). But no man knows these things of his own imagination. These things are revealed to us line upon line.

It is essential to embrace the light and truth we receive with action. This is how we are converted unto the Lord. This is how we lay hold of every good thing.

Learning **how** to grow by never saying "I have enough," prepares us to **become** more and more: to become a saint.

CHAPTER 12

Becoming more and more opens the windows of heaven by receiving line upon line. As we continue to grow, our faith and our knowledge increases, and we are then prepared to come to know our Lord. He will then continue to give us instruction as He did with Paul.

Again, as covered previously, to be prepared for knowing the Lord, we have to study and know the word of God. His word must be fulfilled. When we're in harmony with His word, we're guided back to His presence.

This chapter teaches the results of living a consecrated life. Consecrating your life is to pray to the Father, that He will enhance your incomings and outgoings for the welfare of your soul (see 2 Nephi 32:9). As mentioned earlier, it is to follow the guidance received after asking, "Lord, what wilt thou have me to do?"

Living a consecrated life will lead us to the Lord, Jesus Christ. He will then prepare us to meet our Maker.

Step 4: What to become? Repeat!

Receive and Become More

I said unto you, feast upon the words of Christ; for behold, the words of Christ will tell you all things what ye should do. Wherefore, now after I have spoken these words, if ye cannot understand them it will be because ye ask not, neither do ye knock; wherefore, ye are not brought into the light, but must perish in the dark. For behold, again I say unto you that if ye will enter in by the way, and receive the Holy Ghost, it will show unto you all things what ye should do. Behold, this is the doctrine of Christ, and there will be no more doctrine given until after he shall manifest himself unto you in the flesh. And when he shall manifest himself unto you in the flesh, the things which he shall say unto you shall ye observe to do. (2 Nephi 32:3-6)

Becoming a disciple of Christ is the only way to prepare to meet God. Christ is the way to finding peace in this world, and eternal life in the world to come (see D&C 59:23). We must, therefore, seek after Him by studying His word and by asking "Lord, what wilt Thou have me do?" We will then be given instruction from on High.

The following two quotes help us to see things as they really are by giving us vision of what our *mark* should be:

People who despise plainness are apt to despise the prophets because prophets speak plainly. People can become absorbed in sophisticated and complex things just so long before they become blind to the simple things. People who are looking beyond the mark will miss seeing what they most need to see. They will finally get the desires of their heart and will be delivered over to things "they cannot understand, because they desired it" (Jacob 4:14). How important, by contrast, it is for us to desire to be taught by the Spirit so that we can understand "things as they really are and as they really will be." People who look beyond the mark are clearly not without sight. They can see, but it is what they choose to look at (or for) that causes a lack of vision. It might be likened to ... a basketball player taking his eyes off the basket and missing an easy layup because he glances at a hotdog vendor in the stands; ... or those who were too busy staring in search of a political liberator and missed the Messiah. (Maxwell 1978, 54).

And,

"No amount of searching, if it consists of "looking beyond the mark," will produce a true vision of reality. The "mark" is Christ! To look beyond that mark is to fail fatally in perception. And without such perception, there will be no solutions, for without vision, the people perish. (Maxwell 1982, 113).

When our eye of faith is on "the mark," we seek to become one with Christ. Adhering to what we learn of Him will open the door for us to become acquainted with Him. He will teach us all things and lead us to God the Father.

It is our purpose, while in this school of life, to draw near to God and to know Him again. Notice I didn't say, to know *of* the Father, but to know the Father. To know Him we must draw near to Him by learning His word, which must be fulfilled, and living accordingly. This is the ultimate journey of fulfillment and holiness.

This chapter teaches us that by coming to know our Maker, through His Son Jesus Christ, we are enlightened and receive more than a skyscraper full of riches. We are to receive all the Father has. As the Savior taught, "And this is life eternal, that they might know thee the only true God, and Jesus Christ, whom thou hast sent" (John 17:3).

What does eternal life look like? It is to be an heir with Christ to all the Father has. The following is an explanation of eternal life from Joseph Smith—a man who saw God face to face,

> *Here, then, is eternal life—to know the only wise and true God; and you have got to learn how to be gods yourselves, and to be kings and priests to God, . . . by going from one small degree to another, and from a small capacity to a great one; from grace to grace, from exaltation to exaltation, until you attain to the resurrection of the dead, and are able to dwell in everlasting burnings, and to sit in glory, as do those who sit enthroned in everlasting power...*

(The righteous who have died) shall rise again to dwell in everlasting burnings in immortal glory, not to sorrow, suffer, or die any more, but they shall be heirs of God and joint heirs with Jesus Christ. What is it? To inherit the same power, the same glory and the same exaltation, until you arrive at the station of a god, and ascend the throne of eternal power, the same as those who have gone before. (Smith 2007, 221-222).

In our journey for seeking our divine potential, we discovered the important steps:

1. We saw **what** a saint is (chapter 9).
2. We saw **why** being a saint is important (chapter 10).
3. We saw **how** growth is essential—the tree continues to increase (chapter 11).
4. We saw **what becomes a saint**—one who receives more and more (chapter 12).

In the next section, we learn more about how to prepare to meet our Maker.

SECTION 4

By now, you've become accustomed to the 4-step journey. Here is a recap of the previous sections and of what is to come:

1. In the first section, we learned **what** we are to seek—wisdom—in order to obtain holiness. We also covered how using wisdom to exclusively obtain riches falls short of fulfillment. Rather, we are to become one with Father that we may do good with the riches we receive.

2. In section 2, we learned **why**. We must align our desires with the Lord's word because His word must be fulfilled. In so doing, we are tried to purge the dross from our desires and, in turn, we can prove the words of God to see their fruits. Through our trials, we receive clarity, including further light and truth. With this intelligence, we see with an eye of faith.

3. Section 3 covered **how** we can convert from our fallen state to a divine state, even becoming a saint, a process that lifts our thoughts and ways to those like the Father's thoughts and ways. This allows us to increase more and more unto meeting Deity.

4. In this section 4, we will cover the significance of meeting Deity, **what one must become** and receive to partake of God's fruits. And the power of our choice to lay hold of every good thing unto Moksha, even salvation. It's about being pure as He is pure and meeting Him face to face.

Live What You Know that You May Know More ... Even God the Father!

For of him unto whom much is given much is required ... (D&C 82:3).

Years ago, I heard a folk tale about two men who appeared at the pearly gates to be interviewed for entrance into the kingdom of heaven. Both were interviewed. One was asked to say what he knew of Christ. To which a long dissertation was given about Christ's life as taught in the New Testament. Then the other man came into the office, only to fall upon his knees and proclaim, "Oh, Lord, my God." The moral of the story is we can know about something or we can know something. And when it comes to the weightier matters of life, it is essential that we know as we are known.

The true heritage and potential of man. Since every living thing follows the pattern of its parentage, are we to suppose that God had some other strange pattern in mind for His offspring? Surely we, His children, are not, in the language of science, a different species than He is. What is in error, then, when we use the term Godhood to describe the ultimate destiny of mankind? We may now be young in our progression—juvenile, even infantile, compared with God. Nevertheless, in the eternities to come, if we are worthy, we may be like unto Him, enter His presence, "see as [we] are seen, and know as [we] are known," and receive a "fullness" (Packer 1984, para. 37-38).

We are the offspring of Deity, and to fulfill our potential, we must continue to grow by living what we know. Then by and by, we'll come to know the doctrine of Christ. As we learn and live this doctrine, we'll be prepared to meet Him and His Father. Meeting Deity is the purpose of life. "For behold, this life is the time for men to prepare to meet God; yea, behold the day of this life is the day for men to perform their labors" (Alma 34:32).

Theophany—seeing God face to face—does not have to be a one-time event. Once graced with such privileges one can be ministered unto from time to time (see Jacob 7:5). Now, I'm not talking about being like the first man in the folktale who only knew about Him. I'm talking about living the doctrine of Christ that you may become pure as He is pure, even holy without spot.

In the next chapter of this last section, we'll see the power of knowing as you are known.

CHAPTER 13

In this chapter, we discuss the ramifications of living what we know. I have referred to the phrase "pure as He is pure." To obtain purity, we must be filled with the love of God. Here is where the phrase comes from:

> *Charity is the pure love of Christ, and it endureth forever; and whoso is found possessed of it at the last day, it shall be well with him. Wherefore, my beloved brethren, pray unto the Father with all the energy of heart, that ye may be filled with this love, which he hath bestowed upon all who are true followers of his Son, Jesus Christ; that ye may become the sons of God; that when he shall appear we shall be like him, for we shall see him as he is; that we may have this hope; that we may be purified even as he is pure. Amen. (Moroni 7:47-48)*

I love this notion of being pure as He is pure. This teaches the significance of living the word of God and not just knowing it. As we live the word, we become more and more, as discussed.

Planting the seed or word of God will lead to a tree of life growth within our soul. As we continue to grow, we'll display the fruits of God. In so doing others will know Him by knowing us.

This chapter is about knowing. It's about living what you know that others may know what you know by your word and deed.

Step 1: What?

To Know as You Are Known

To know and not to do is really not to know. (Covey 2004, 12.).

On this earth, in this school of life, we are given the opportunity to be an agent for Christ or not. To be His disciple is to use agency appropriately. Again, we are not just knowing of Him, but being like Him.

We can know what Christ teaches is true by living what He teaches (see John 7:17). And as a result, we partake of the divine nature and the fruits of the Spirit. We become like Him now and forever.

Let us join Christ in becoming one with the Father that we may,

Dwell in [God's] presence ... and ... see as [we] are seen, and know as [we] are known, having received of his fullness and of his grace; And he makes [us] equal in power, and in might, and in dominion. (D&C 76:94-95)

So **what** we must know is to know our Father, not just know about Him, but truly know him. And in so doing, we live so that others know what we know.

Throughout this book, I have used the plainest language I know. Each reader will comprehend things according to his or her language and understanding (see 2 Nephi 31:3).

In the next chapter, we'll discuss **why** we must come to know Him: we can embrace the beauty of receiving a greater portion of God's word, or the opposite, receiving a lesser portion. It's up to us!

CHAPTER 14

In our last chapter, we spelled out the power of living what you know that others may know what you know, even God. We also concluded with a scripture about the blessing that comes from hearkening to the word of the Lord to become one with Him.

In this chapter, we discuss two options: Growth vs. Death. To plant a seed on good ground and to nurture it is to continue and receive more and more growth unto eternal life, whereas if you were to plant on the hardened ground, the seed could not take root and would perish.

Step 2: Why?

Lesser Portion vs. Greater Portion of the Word

And therefore, he that will harden his heart, the same receiveth the lesser portion of the word; and he that will not harden his heart, to him is given the greater portion of the word, until it is given unto him to know the mysteries of God until he know them in full. (Alma 12:10)

As an agent of Christ, we are given to know the mysteries of God. Whereas, if we choose not to be an agent of Christ by rejecting the mysteries we have, then that which was given will be taken away. Thus,

They that will harden their hearts, to them is given the lesser portion of the word until they know nothing concerning his mysteries; and then they are taken captive by the devil, and led by his will down to destruction. Now this is what is meant by the chains of hell. (Alma 12:10-11)

With obedience to universal laws and principles, even the mysteries of God, we're empowered with further light and truth. And with that light and truth comes greater power to act for ourselves and a fullness of the blessings offered to those who become one with the Christ.

And if a person gains more knowledge and intelligence in this life through his diligence and obedience than another, he will have so much the advantage in the world to come. There is a law, irrevocably decreed in heaven before the foundations of this world, upon which all blessings are predicated—And when we obtain any blessing from God, it is by obedience to that law upon which it is predicated. (D&C 130:19-21)

Continue to learn universal laws and live by them. Continue to increase your intelligence. I'm not referring to IQ, but rather suggesting you stock up on the divine currency of intelligence, which is the glory of God (see D&C 93:36).

In this chapter, we have laid out **why** we should place emphasis on growth by receiving more and more of the word of God until we know them in full.

In the next chapter, we will see **how** to live the fruits of the word we plant in our lives.

CHAPTER 15

We have covered the importance of obeying what we know that we may know more. In this chapter, we see the power of living the word of God.

Step 3: How?

Planting God's Word = Partaking of His fruits

It is a well-known fact that one comes to finally BELIEVE whatever one repeats to one's self, whether the statement be true or false. If we repeat a lie over and over, we will eventually accept the lie as truth. Moreover, we will BELIEVE it to be the truth. Each of us is what we are because of the DOMINATING THOUGHTS which we permit to occupy our mind. Thoughts which we deliberately place in our own mind, and encourage with sympathy, and with which we mix any one of or more of the emotions, constitute the motivating forces which direct and control every movement, act, and deed! Comes, now, a very significant statement of truth: THOUGHTS WHICH ARE MIXED WITH ANY OF THE FEELINGS OF EMOTIONS CONSTITUTE A "MAGNETIC" FORCE WHICH ATTRACTS OTHER SIMILAR, OR RELATED THOUGHTS. A thought thus "magnetized" with emotion may be compared to a seed which, when planted in fertile soil, germinates, grows, and multiplies itself over and over until that which was originally one small seed becomes countless millions of seeds of the SAME KIND! (Hill 2007, 48-49).

What seeds will you plant? Seeds of light and truth that bring the fruits of the Spirit, including joy and happiness? Or seeds of darkness that bring misery and destruction?

As offspring to Deity, we are beings of intelligence, like unto God. It is written,

The glory of God is intelligence, or, in other words, light and truth. Light and truth forsake that evil one. Every spirit of man was innocent in the beginning; and God having redeemed man from the fall, men became again, in their infant state, innocent before God. And that wicked one cometh and taketh away light and truth, through disobedience, from the children of men, and because of the tradition of their fathers. (D&C 93:36-39)

When we use our agency properly, we cleave unto more and more intelligence as it is presented to us, and we forsake lesser things. Whereas, the adversary (an enemy to all righteousness) strives to take away our light and truth. And the only way he can do this is through our disobedience to light and truth.

This removing of light can be done directly or indirectly, meaning we could simply disobey something that we know is right, or we may have been taught a false tradition from previous generations. The adversary will use all he can to act upon us. For example, he appeared unto one man as follows,

> But behold, the devil hath deceived me; for he appeared unto me in the form of an angel, and said unto me: Go and reclaim this people, for they have all gone astray after an unknown God. And he said unto me: There is no God; yea, and he taught me that which I should say. And I have taught his words; and I taught them because they were pleasing unto the carnal mind; and I taught them, even until I had much success, insomuch that I verily believed that they were true; and for this cause I withstood the truth, even until I have brought this great curse upon me. (Alma 30:53)

However, when our eye is single to the glory of God, and we continue to cleave unto intelligence as it is presented to us, we are filled with power from on High. We will have a change of heart and be a partaker of the divine nature. In so doing, we will bear righteous fruits and have "power to overcome all things which are not ordained of him" (D&C 50:35).

When we bear righteous fruits for others to partake of, we empower them to remember God. We act as God's love to His children. Let's love our fellowman that they may learn God's love and in return begin to love Him too (see 1 John 4:19; Luke 10:27-28).

What fruit should we bear? "The fruit of the Spirit [which] is love, joy, peace, longsuffering, gentleness, goodness, faith, meekness, temperance" (Galatians 5:22-23). An understanding of **how** to prepare to meet Deity and desiring to bear these righteous fruits leads to the next chapter of **what we become.**

CHAPTER 16

In college, I had a wise professor (Joseph Fielding McConkie) who taught with power and authority. Here are two of the nuggets he taught me:

1. The older I get, the more I realize there are no accidents in life.

2. Like an insurance agent represents a company or many companies, we too are agents. In fact, we are agents for Christ, or we are not, there are no other options.

It is no accident that you have read this book. You and I have been called to "the more weighty matters" in life (D&C 117:8). Acquiring things is but a drop in the bucket of life. However, living what we know that we may know God is the weightiest matter. Knowing God is salvation.

There is only one way to know God—face to face—it is through coming to know His Son Jesus Christ. Which gift is preceded by laying hold of every good thing. Let us, therefore, choose to be agents of Christ.

Step 4: What to become? Repeat!

Acting for ourselves

"Wherefore, the Lord God gave unto man that he should act for himself. Wherefore, man could not act for himself save it should be that he was enticed by the one or the other" (2 Nephi 2:16).

With our agency, we can act for ourselves or be acted upon. When we cleave unto the fruit of the Spirit as it is presented to us, we are being an agent for Christ. When we cower away from the divine nature by following the lusts of the carnal nature, we are being acted upon and lose power to act for ourselves.

I admonish you to draw near unto God by laying hold of every good thing. Remember to,

Draw near unto [Him] and [He] will draw near unto you; seek [Him] diligently and ye shall find [Him]; ask, and ye shall receive; knock, and it shall be opened unto you. Whatsoever ye ask the Father in [Christ's] name it shall be given unto you, that is expedient for you; And if ye ask anything that is not expedient for you, it shall turn unto your condemnation. (D&C 88:63-65)

Seek, therefore, the words of life. In so doing, you'll be filled with more and more light and truth. This enlightenment will teach you what to ask for. It will empower you to act in righteousness and purge your soul of any dross that may have held you back.

By studying and adhering to the words of life, you'll be prepared to meet your Maker. To do this, your eye of faith must be single to your Father's glory. It is written,

> *And if your eye be single to my glory, your whole bodies shall be filled with light, and there shall be no darkness in you; and that body which is filled with light comprehendeth all things. Therefore, sanctify yourselves that your minds become single to God, and the days will come that you shall see him; for he will unveil his face unto you, and it shall be in his own time, and in his own way, and according to his own will. (D&C 88:67-68)*

Throughout this book, we've discussed a 4-step journey to holiness. This process culminates with coming to know Deity face to face. But like the prophets of old who have known Him, this is not the end. They spent the remainder of their days helping others to know what they know. This was there spreading of the good news, even the gospel. The following sums up the power of living a life of holiness,

> *The most effective way to preach the gospel is through example. If we live according to our beliefs, people will notice. If the countenance of Jesus Christ shines in our lives, if we are joyful and at peace with the world, people will want to know why. One of the greatest sermons ever pronounced on [living what you know] is this simple thought attributed to Saint Francis of Assisi: "Preach the gospel at all times and if necessary, use words." Opportunities to do so are all around us. (Uchtdorf 2011, 70)*

As agents of Christ,

We talk of Christ, we rejoice in Christ, we preach of Christ, we prophesy of Christ, and we write according to our prophecies, that our children may know to what source they may look for a remission of their sins. (2 Nephi 25:26)

Choosing to lay hold of every good thing leads us to know Christ and opens the door for us to be holy. Being holy, pure as He is pure, prepares us to fulfill our purpose in life to know God face to face. When we do this, we are acting for ourselves rather than being acted upon by the lusts of the flesh.

Conclusion

The 4-Step Journey to Holiness leads to a life beyond worldly riches! If one desires, he or she will obtain riches, too. The crux of holiness is to have an eye single to the Glory of God. It is to seek for divine currency that will pass with us to the next life, even the character of holiness and all the attributes of godliness.

In conclusion, I turn to a quote about stewardship. We are held accountable for how we live what we know. Do those who know us or read our material know the Divine? If not, we could be in danger of "misdirecting another's life."

Winston Churchill said of military secrets that in wartime it is necessary for the truth to be surrounded by a bodyguard of lies. But [universal] truths must always be "fair as the sun, clear as the moon," being set forth plainly, straightforwardly, and simply. There is too much chance of miscommunication and too much risk of having someone deflected from discipleship because of misunderstanding. To give a tourist wrong directions is inconvenient, but to misdirect an individual's life is intolerable. (Maxwell 1978. 108,)

It has been a pleasure sharing this experience with you. I write from the heart of my understanding. I challenge you to "Prove all things; hold fast that which is good" (1 Thessalonians 5:21).

As children of God, you and I are given the opportunity in this life to prepare to meet Him. We are beings of light and truth, even intelligences. Remember, "Intelligence cleaveth unto intelligence; wisdom receiveth wisdom; truth embraceth truth; virtue loveth virtue; light cleaveth unto light" (D&C 88:40).

Prove what I have spoken of by living it. Then, by the fruits, you will know if it is true. Remember,

> *If any man will do his will, he shall know of the doctrine, whether it be of God, or whether I speak of myself. He that speaketh of himself seeketh his own glory: but he that seeketh his glory that sent him, the same is true, and no unrighteousness is in him. (John 7:17-18)*

We are sent here to see if we will use our agency for Christ, or not. All things that come into our lives are designed to draw us unto God. For it is written, "And we will prove them herewith, to see if they will do all things whatsoever the Lord their God shall command them" (Abraham 3:25).

Let us embrace our trials and learn from them by turning our burden over to the Lord. He desires to bless us and to endow us with further light and truth. This enlightenment will purge us of our imperfections. He desires to "pour down" knowledge from heaven, if we will but receive it.

Look at the imagery of the following verse of scripture,

How long can rolling waters remain impure? What power shall stay the heavens? As well might man stretch forth his puny arm to stop the Missouri river in its decreed course, or to turn it up stream, as to hinder the Almighty from pouring down knowledge from heaven upon the heads of the Latter-day Saints. (D&C 121:33)

No one, nor any army, can stop the word of God from being fulfilled. Discover the word of God in your life. Seek to understand and live by it. Study and implement it. Prove it in your life and become a partaker of the fruits of the Spirit, including the divine nature.

Continue to follow the 4-step journey to holiness:

1. Be quick to observe with an inquisitive mind.

2. Allow your innate desire to be reconciled to God to guide you.

3. Lay hold of every good thing, and you will be filled with spiritual gifts for contribution.

4. Tap into God's power to become one with Him, even holy without spot.

References

Benson, Ezra Taft "Think on Christ," *Ensign*, April 1984. Accessed February 20, 2016, https://www.lds.org/ensign/1984/04/think-on-christ?lang=eng

Benson, Ezra Taft. "Jesus Christ—Gifts and Expectations," *Ensign*, December 1988. Accessed February 20, 2016, https://www.lds.org/ensign/1988/12/jesus-christ-gifts-and-expectations?lang=eng

Caldwell, C. Max. "A Mighty Change," in *The Book of Mormon: Alma, the Testimony of the Word*, ed. Monte S. Nyman and Charles D. Tate Jr. Provo, UT: Religious Studies Center, Brigham Young University, 1992, 27–46. Accessed February 20, 2016, https://rsc.byu.edu/archived/book-mormon-alma-testimony-word/3-mighty-change.

Church of Jesus Christ of Latter-day Saints (LDS). *Preach My Gospel*, (Salt Lake City: author, 2004).

Covey, Stephen R. *7 Habits of Highly Effective People: Restoring the Character Ethic*, (New York: Free Press, 2004).

Covey, Stephen R. *7 Habits of Highly Effective People: Restoring the Character Ethic*, (New York: Simon & Schuster, 1989).

Deiter F. Uchtdorf, "Waiting on the Road to Damascus," *Ensign*, May 2011. Accessed February, 2016, https://www.lds.org/ensign/2011/05/waiting-on-the-road-to-damascus?lang=eng

Doctrine and Covenants (D&C). (Salt Lake City: The Church of Jesus Christ of Latter-day Saints, 2013). Accessed February 20, 2016, http://scriptures.byu.edu/.

Ecker, T. Harv. *Secrets of the Millionaire Mind: Mastering the Inner Game of Wealth*, (HarperCollins e-book, 2009).

Eyring, Henry B. "Mountains to Climb," *Ensign*, May 2012. Accessed February 20, 2016. https://www.lds.org/ensign/2012/05/mountains-to-climb?lang=eng.

Gandhi, Mohandas K. *An Autobiography: The Story of My Experiments with Truth*, (Boston: Beacon Press, 1993).

Hill, Napoleon. *Outwitting the Devil*, (New York: Sterling, 2011).

Hill, Napoleon. *Think and Grow Rich: The Original Version, Restored and Revised*, compiled by Ross Cornwell (Aventine Press, 2007).

Hinckley, Gordon B. "Excerpts from Recent Addresses of President Gordon B. Hinckley," *Ensign*, August 1998. Accessed February 20, 2016, https://www.lds.org/ensign/1998/08/excerpts-from-recent-addresses-of-president-gordon-b-hinckley?lang=eng

Holland, Jeffrey R. "Tongue of Angels," *Ensign*, May 2007. Accessed February 20, 2016, https://www.lds.org/ensign/2007/05/the-tongue-of-angels?lang=eng

Kimball, Spencer W. "Give Me This Mountain," *Ensign*, November 1979.

Lewis, C.S. *Mere Christianity*, (Haper San Francisco, 2001).

Maxwell, Neal A. "The Disciple Scholar," in *On Becoming a Disciple Scholar*, compiled by Henry B. Eyring, (Salt Lake City: Deseret Book Company, 1995).

Maxwell, Neal A. *Even As I Am*, (Salt Lake City: Deseret Book Company, 1982).

Maxwell, Neal A. *Things as They Really Are*, (Salt Lake City: Deseret Book Company, 1978).

McConkie, Bruce R. *Doctrinal New Testament Commentary*, vol. 1. (Salt Lake City: Deseret Book Company, 1965), 770.

McConkie, Joseph Fielding. *Prophets & Prophecy*, (Salt Lake City: Bookcraft, 1988).

Packer, Boyd K. "The Pattern of Our Parentage," *Ensign*, November 1984.

Pearce, Virginia H. *Respect, Equality, & Recognizing the Spirit*, (BYU-Idaho Devotional, 15 April 1997), Accessed February 20, 2016, https://byui-media.ldscdn.org/byui_ft/devo_audio/1997_04_15_ADV_Pearce.mp3

Pearl of Great Price, (Salt Lake City: The Church of Jesus Christ of Latter-day Saints, 2013).

Pritchett, Price. *You²: a High-Velocity Formula for Multiplying your Personal Effectiveness in Quantum Leaps*, (Pritchett & Associates, 2012).

Proctor, Bob. *You Were Born Rich*, (Scottsdale, AZ: LifeSuccess

Productions, 2002).p

Schwartz, David. *The Magic of Thinking Big*, (New York: Simon & Schuster, 1987).

Smith, Joseph. *Lectures on Faith*, (Salt Lake City: Deseret Book Company, 1985).

Smith, Joseph. *Teachings of Presidents of the Church: Joseph Smith*, (Salt Lake City: The Church of Jesus Christ of Latter-day Saints, 2007).

The Book of Mormon: Another Testament of Jesus Christ. (Salt Lake City: The Church of Jesus Christ of Latter-day Saints, 2013).

Uchtdorf, Deiter F. "The Best Time to Plant a Tree," *Ensign*, January 2014, 4.

Webster, Noah. *American Dictionary of the English Language*, s.v. "saint." (San Francisco: Foundation for American Christian Education, 2014), vol. II.

Young, Brigham. *Journal of Discourses*, Vol. 8 (London: Latter-day Saints' Book Depot, 1860), 334-335.

About the Author
and Thank You!

I am the proud father, sealed to my children and beautiful wife for time and all eternity. My wife and I met at a service project while attending Brigham Young University. Afterwards, I graduated with a BA with university honors in American Studies.

To learn more about me, you're welcome to check out my blog: KentEynerNielsen.com.

Thank you for purchasing and reading this book. The best compliment you could give me would be to give this book to others and discuss how it has impacted you. If you have felt moved by the teachings in this book, I welcome you to leave a review on Amazon.

I hope this book has served as a catalyst to draw you closer to the Lord.

90704098R00074

Made in the USA
Columbia, SC
10 March 2018